Presented by
FRANCO
l. H. W
31 July 1972

PELICAN BOOKS

Pelican Library of Business and Management

CORPORATE STRATEGY

H. Igor Ansoff is Professor of Industrial Administration at the Graduate School, Carnegie Institute of Technology. He was appointed to this post in 1963.

A graduate of Stevens Institute of Technology and Brown University, Dr Ansoff worked for the RAND Corporation as a project officer and with Lockheed Electronics Company, where he became vice-president and general manager of the Industrial Technology Division.

Dr Ansoff has written many management articles, some of which have been presented to professional organizations, and others published in periodicals such as *Harvard Business Review*, *Review of Management and Economics*, and *Management Technology*.

D0048074

H. IGOR ANSOFF

CORPORATE STRATEGY

AN ANALYTIC APPROACH TO BUSINESS POLICY FOR GROWTH AND EXPANSION

PENGUIN BOOKS

Penguin Books Ltd, Harmondsworth, Middlesex, England
Penguin Books Australia Ltd, Ringwood, Victoria, Australia

—

First published in the U.S.A. by McGraw-Hill 1965
Published in Great Britain by Penguin Books 1968
Reprinted 1970

—

Copyright © McGraw-Hill, 1965, 1968

—

Made and printed in Great Britain
by Richard Clay (The Chaucer Press) Ltd,
Bungay, Suffolk
Set in Monotype Times

TO THE MEMORY OF ROBERT E. GROSS

Contents

Preface

THIS book is concerned with *business strategy formulation* in the social-economic environment of the United States. The concepts and methodology presented are applicable to other environments and other types of institutions, However, the approach, the terminology, the examples, and the concepts are all derived from the American business scene.

This book is concerned with *management*, the active process of determining and guiding the course of a firm toward its objectives. In contrast to more common descriptive theories used in the economic theory, the interest is normative: we seek to develop a practically useful series of concepts and procedures which managers can use to manage.

Management of a business firm is a very large complex of activities which consists of analysis, decisions, communication, leadership, motivation, measurement, and control. Of these, we single out the process of decision making, since it is the corner stone of successful management. Peter Drucker has said, 'The end-products of management are decisions and actions.' Decisions, whether explicitly or implicitly arrived at, precede every action. Our interest is in the characteristics of these decisions, regardless of the organizational process by which they are made: through an authoritarian management structure, through participative management, or by default.

Our interest is in a particular part of the total 'space' of decisions which confronts a business manager. These are the *strategic decisions*. Presently such decisions will be defined more carefully. For the time being let us describe them as decisions on what kind of business the firm should seek to be in.

In viewing the problem of strategic decisions the approach is analytic. Management was born and developed as an art. Early in the twentieth century, pioneers like F. W. Taylor, Elton Mayo, and Henri Fayol began to apply science to management. The post-World War II period has seen a blossoming of applications of operations research and management science to problems of the firm. Historical progress has been from the 'inside out'. Taylor, Mayo, and their generation concerned themselves with problems of individual and group productivity within the manufacturing organization. Post-war efforts have spread to a wide range of internal operating problems of the firm. Analytic approaches to the external or strategic problems of the firm have come last. Over the past ten years a number of writers have provided *partial* analytical insights into strategic business problems. The purpose of this book is to synthesize and unify these into an overall analytic approach to solving the *total* strategic problem of the firm.

Finally, we have attempted to make the analytic framework *practical*. This calls for a compromise between mathematical precision on the one hand and realism in the problem statement on the other. The compromise is consistently made in favour of the latter. What has emerged is a qualitative–quantitative framework stated in business language and directly usable for solving real-world business problems. In fact, the framework is an outgrowth of several concrete problems which the author has helped solve.

Methodologically, the 'scientific' method of operations research and management science is not wholly applicable to the strategic problem. In fact, the method falls short in several important respects. A partial result of this book, therefore, is a *new* methodology which appears more suitable for problems of the type considered here.

In summary, this book provides a practical method for strategic decision making within a business firm. It is addressed to working managers responsible for such decisions: the chairman of the board, board members, the chairman, the chief financial officer, and the development and planning staffs which report to them. Drafts of this book have proved useful in teaching graduate and executive training courses in the area commonly known as 'business policy'. It is my hope that other teachers and students of management will find it similarly useful.

The chapters in the book have been arranged to enable a busy executive to become acquainted with the concepts and the general approach without becoming involved in the technical details of its development. Such readers may wish to proceed from Chapter 7 directly to Chapter 10.

Acknowledgements

A BOOK which attempts to marry theory and practice owes its debt to two backgrounds. On the practical side my great debt is to the late Robert E. Gross, former Chairman of Lockheed Aircraft Corporation, who taught me what I know about business strategy. My thanks and affection also to C. A. Barker, Jr, Director and former Senior Vice-chairman of Lockheed, and G. B. Brashears, Honorary Director, at whose respective knees I began to understand the intricacies of business evaluation and finance. D. J. Haughton, President of Lockheed, has been unfailingly understanding and patient as he guided me in applying a new strategy to practice. This acknowledgement would swell to unmanageable proportions if I were to list all other friends and associates in Lockheed and outside who indirectly contributed to this book.

On the theoretical side, my major debt is to a group of collaborators who jointly gave birth to much of what is in this book. These are Theodore A. Andersen, Don Lebell, Frank E. Norton, and J. F. Weston. Don Lebell had the brilliant original insights which prevailed after the rest of us did our best to disprove them. Fred Weston has contributed more than I had any right to ask. Except for other commitments, he would have been a welcome co-author of this book.

I doubt that this book would have been started and written had it not been for the insistence and prodding of Nancy Johnson, an executive secretary par excellence. My new colleagues at Carnegie Institute of Technology have contributed much to its completion: Dean William R. Dill with his helpful comments and Dean Richard M. Cyert with his generosity and support. Miss Judith Brunclik did an outstanding job of managing and typing the manuscript.

In the last analysis, the book belongs forty per cent to me and sixty per cent to my wife, who has cheerfully accepted and encouraged a seven-day work week.

H.I.A.

13

CHAPTER 1

Structure of Business Decisions

... The strategic aim of a business [is] to earn a return on capital, and if in any particular case the return in the long run is not satisfactory, then the deficiency should be corrected or the activity abandoned for a more favorable one.

ALFRED P. SLOAN, JR

THE PROBLEM

As every experienced executive knows, a major part of a manager's time is occupied in a daily process of making numerous and diverse decisions. The demands on the decision maker's time always seem to exceed his capacity; decisions of great potential import come mixed with trivial but time-consuming demands; the nature of decisions is multifaceted and continually variable. This diversity generally tends to increase with the level of responsibility and becomes particularly pronounced for the top executive of the firm. On a single day he may be called upon to decide on a future course of the firm's business, to reconcile an organizational conflict between two executives, and to resolve a host of day-to-day operating problems.

In seeking to understand this very complex decision process we can proceed along two complementary lines. The first, and by far the more ambitious one, is to discover how people in general and executives in particular, make decisions, either individually or in groups. Given the alternatives and their consequences, what kind of group interactions are they involved in, what mental process do they go through, and what rules do they apply in arriving at the preferred choice? This direction, which goes under the general name of *decision theory*, has received much attention for many years from diverse scientific disciplines: philosophy, psychology, mathematics, and economics. It is a testimony to the difficulty of this problem that all of these efforts have produced very few practical results to date.

The other direction is to study the alternatives and their consequences to seek an understanding of the nature and the structure of decisions – to identify the problem, to enumerate and define the controllable and uncontrollable variables, to establish relationships among them, to single out important decisions and to prescribe rules for arriving at them. This is a somewhat less ambitious task, for it does not attempt to penetrate the decision maker's mind. Rather, it seeks to study the nature of his job and thus improve decision making through improving his insights into the antecedents and the consequences of major decisions. Instead of studying the mind of the manager, this approach explores the business firm.

Study of the firm has been the long-time concern of the economics profession. Unfortunately for our present purpose, the so-called *microeconomic* theory of the firm, which occupies much of the economists' thought and attention, sheds relatively little light on decision-making processes in a real-world firm.[1] * A very recent significant contribution to understanding decision processes has been made by Cyert and March. They have formulated a *behavioral* theory of the firm[2] which combines economic analysis with social behaviour and is addressed explicitly to business decisions within a firm. However, the class of decisions studied by them is limited and different from the class of interest to us, namely, strategic decisions.

This book is in the tradition of the microeconomic and the behavioral theories in the sense that it is primarily concerned with the nature of the firm and not with the decision maker's mind. We shall have much to say about the characteristics of decisions and the process of search for alternatives and very little, beyond a brief review of the current knowledge, about the utility function applied at the ultimate 'moment of truth' in selecting the preferred alternative.

Since there is no adequate theory of the strategic decision process, we have to start by constructing our own model of the firm. The purpose of this chapter is first to outline such a model and then to single out the principal classes of business decisions. Following this we shall discuss some special characteristics of one of these classes – the strategic decisions – which is the core subject of this book.

* Superior numbers refer to references at the end of the book.

CLASSES OF DECISIONS

The adjective 'business' has traditionally meant that the firm is an *economically* or 'money' motivated *purposive* social organization. This implies that a set of objectives or purposes can be identified in most firms, either in explicit form as a part of the firm's business plan, or implicitly through past history and individual motivations of the key personnel. Traditionally the measure of success in a business firm has been profit – the excess of returns to the firm over the costs incurred – and it is this measure that has distinguished a business firm from other forms of social organization such as the government, the church, the armed forces, nonprofitmaking foundations, etc.

As will be seen in Chapter 3, the role of profitability as the corner stone of business has recently been subjected to sharp questioning. Further, measurement of profitability presents some difficult theoretical as well as practical problems. However, for the purpose of discussing business decisions we need only what mathematicians would call a 'weak' assumption, namely, that, however measured and however variable, a set of objectives can be ascribed to each firm, and that this set is the major guidepost in the decision process.

The second major characteristic which is essential to an understanding of decision making is that a firm seeks its objectives through the medium of profit and, more specifically, through conversion of its resources into goods and/or services and then obtaining a return on these by *selling* them to customers. There are three types of basic resources: physical (inventory, plant), monetary (money, credit), and human. All three are used up in the conversion process: plant becomes obsolete, money gets spent, and executives get old. In this respect, survival of the firm depends on profit; unless profits are generated and used for replacement of resources, the firm will eventually run down.

From a decision viewpoint the overall problem of the business of the firm is *to configure and direct the resource-conversion process in such way as to optimize the attainment of the objectives.* Since this calls for a great many distinct and different decisions, a study of the overall decision process can be facilitated by dividing the total decision 'space' into several distinct categories. Our approach will be to construct three categories called respectively *strategic*, *administrative*, and *operating*, each related to a different aspect of the resource-conversion process.

Operating decisions usually absorb the bulk of the firm's energy and attention. The object is to maximize the efficiency of the firm's resource-conversion process, or, in more conventional language, to maximize profitability of current operations. The major decision areas are resource allocation (budgeting) among functional areas and product lines, scheduling of operations, supervision of performance, and applying control actions. The key decisions involve pricing, establishing marketing strategy, setting production schedules and inventory levels, and deciding on relative expenditures in support of R & D (research and development), marketing, and operations.

Strategic decisions * are primarily concerned with external, rather than internal, problems of the firm and specifically with selection of the product-mix which the firm will produce and the markets to which it will sell. To use an engineering term, the strategic problem is concerned with establishing an 'impedance match' between the firm and its environment or, in more usual terms, it is the problem of deciding what business the firm is in and what kinds of businesses it will seek to enter.

Specific questions addressed in the strategic problem are: what are the firm's objectives and goals; should the firm seek to diversify, in what areas, how vigorously; and how should the firm develop and exploit its present product-market position.

A very important feature of the overall business decision process becomes accentuated in the strategic problem. This is the fact that a large majority of decisions must be made within the framework of a limited total resource. Regardless of how large or small the firm, strategic decisions deal with a choice of resource com-

* Here, we use the term strategic to mean 'pertaining to the relation between the firm and its environment'. This is more specific and different from a more common usage in which 'strategic' denotes 'important'. Depending on its position, the firm may find operating decisions to be more important than strategic ones.

mitments among alternatives; emphasis on current business will preclude diversification, over-emphasis on diversification will lead to neglect of present products. The object is to produce a resource-allocation pattern which will offer the best potential for meeting the firm's objectives.

Administrative decisions are concerned with structuring the firm's resources in a way which creates a maximum performance potential. One part of the administrative problem is concerned with organization: structuring of authority and responsibility relationships, work flows, information flows, distribution channels, and location of facilities. The other part is concerned with acquisition and development of resources: development of raw-material sources, personnel training and development, financing, and acquisition of facilities and equipment.

INTERACTIONS AMONG DECISION CLASSES

The characteristics of the three classes of decisions are summarized in Table 1.1. While distinct, the decisions are interdependent and complementary. The strategic decisions assure that the firm's products and markets are well chosen, that adequate demand exists, and that the firm is capable of capturing a share of the demand. Strategy imposes operating requirements: price–cost decisions, timing of output to meet the demand, responsiveness to changes in customer needs and technological and process characteristics. The administrative structure must provide the climate for meeting these, e.g. a strategic environment which is characterized by frequent and unpredictable demand fluctuations requires that marketing and manufacturing be closely coupled organizationally for rapid response; an environment which is highly technical requires that the research and development department work in close cooperation with sales personnel.

In this sense 'structure follows strategy' – product-market characteristics create operating needs, and these, in turn, determine the structure of authority, responsibility, work flows, and information flows within the firm. A. D. Chandler[3] has illustrated this relationship of strategy and structure through a historical analysis of American business. As the country's economy developed, different strategic opportunities became available to business. As firms took advantage of these opportunities and thus changed their previous strategies, operating inadequacies developed which dictated new forms of organization. Chandler traces the development of the modern concept of centralized policy making with decentralized operations control to its strategic and operating antecedents. Alfred P. Sloan in his memoirs[4] has diagnosed one of the major requirements which strategy has imposed on structure: to organize the firm's management in a way which assures a proper balance of attention between the strategic and operating decisions.

Such balance is difficult to achieve. In most firms everyone in the organization is concerned with a myriad of recurring operating problems. Management from top to bottom continually seeks to improve efficiency, to cut costs, to sell more, to advertise better. Problems are automatically generated at all levels of management, and those which are beyond the scope of lower management authority become the concern of top management. The volume of such decisions is great and constant, particularly because of the need for daily supervision and control. In fact one of the major concerns of top management is to avoid overload by establishing decision priorities and by delegating as much as possible to lower managers.

By contrast, strategic decisions are not self-regenerative; they make no automatic claims on top management attention. Unless actively pursued, they may remain hidden behind the operations problems. Firms are generally very slow in recognizing conditions under which concern with the operating problem must give way to a concern with the strategic. Usually when such conditions occur, operating problems neither cease nor slacken. On the contrary, they appear to intensify. The last promotional campaign has failed to increase sales. Could the advertising approach be wrong? The last cost reduction effort has failed to bring costs in line with prices. Have we taken the proper approach toward increased efficiency? Competition has cut prices to a point below our costs. Should we meet them and go into the red, or should we hold the line?

The immediate demands on management time and effort raised

TABLE 1.1 *Principal Decision Classes in the Firm*

	Strategic	Administrative	Operating
Problem	To select product-market mix which optimizes firm's ROI* potential	To structure firm's resources for optimum performance	To optimize realization of ROI potential
Nature of problem	Allocation of total resources among product-market opportunities	Organization, acquisition, and development of resources	Budgeting of resources among principal functional areas Scheduling resource application and conversion Supervision and control
Key decisions	Objectives and goals Diversification strategy Expansion strategy Administrative strategy Finance strategy Growth method Timing of growth	Organization: structure of information, authority, and responsibility flows Structure of resource-conversion: work flows, distribution system, facilities location Resource acquisition and development: financing, facilities and equipment, personnel, raw materials	Operating objectives and goals Operating levels: production schedules, inventory levels, warehousing, etc. Marketing policies and strategy R & D policies and strategy Control
Key characteristics	Decisions centralized Partial ignorance Decisions non-repetitive Decisions not self-regenerative	Conflict between strategy and operations Conflict between individual and institutional objectives Strong coupling between economic and social variables Decisions triggered by strategic and/or operating problems	Decentralized decisions Risk and uncertainty Repetitive decisions Large volume of decisions Suboptimization forced by complexity Decisions self-regenerative

* ROI stands for 'return on investment' (this concept will be explored fully in Chapter 3).

by such operating problems can readily obscure the fact that the basic ills lie not in the firm but in its environment. Even when a continuous downward trend in profitability or obvious signs of market saturation strongly point to the need to revamp the entire product-market position, a natural tendency is to seek remedies in operational improvements: cost reduction, consolidation, a new advertising manager, and, the most popular remedy of them all, reorganization of the company. And yet the main problem may be that the demand for the firm's products is on a rapid decline.

Since strategic problems are harder to pinpoint, they require special attention. Unless specific provisions are made for concern with strategy, the firm may misplace its effort in pursuit of operating efficiency at times when attention to strategic opportunities (or threats) can produce a more radical and immediate improvement in the firm's performance.

Two kinds of provisions are required. One is to provide an administrative environment in which a proper balance of management attention can be maintained. This is the main subject of Chandler's book. With one exception in Chapter 8 we shall not deal with problems of organization. The other is to provide management with a method of analysis which is focused on the search for strategic decision needs and opportunities. This feature is the cornerstone of the problem-solving method which we shall develop in this book.

It is clear from preceding remarks that a comprehensive theory of decision making within a firm must include the interactions among the major classes of decisions. On the other hand, Table 1.1 suggests that each class has distinctive characteristics and that they are better studied separately. As a first step toward a unified theory, partial theories of the respective operating, administrative, and strategic decision classes must be understood. Cyert and March have made an important contribution to study of the first class; Chandler's work sheds important light on the second. Our purpose in this book is to construct a practical framework for the third. As a step toward a unified theory the final chapter of this book will discuss the role of strategy within the overall structure of decisions.

CHAPTER 2

A Model for Strategic Decisions

There are more things in heaven and earth, Horatio, than are
dreamt of in your philosophy.

WILLIAM SHAKESPEARE

THE PROBLEM

THE end product of strategic decisions is deceptively simple; a
combination of products and markets is selected for the firm.
This combination is arrived at by addition of new product-
markets, divestment from some old ones, and expansion of the
present position. The change from previous posture requires a re-
distribution of the firm's resources – a pattern of divestments and
investments in company acquisitions, product development,
marketing outlets, advertising, etc. At first glance, strategic decisions resemble capital-investment decisions, which deal in a
similar manner with resource allocation to fixed assets and
machinery. Since a well-developed theory is available for capital-
investment decisions, it is useful to start the discussion by review-
ing the applicability of this theory to the strategic problem.

This analysis will show that the resemblance is more superficial
than real and that the differences between the two types of decisions are so great as to require new concepts and methodology of
the strategic problem.

A framework containing such concepts and methodology will
be described at the end of this chapter as an introduction to the
detailed analyses in later chapters.

CAPITAL INVESTMENT THEORY (CIT)*

Capital investment analysis starts with identification and
enumeration of fixed asset and equipment proposals for the next
budget period. For each proposal, positive (revenues) and

* For the sake of brevity, in the following pages we will occasionally use
CIT to denote capital investment theory.

23

negative (costs) cash flows are computed over the life-time of the project. For proper comparison, these flows must be marginal to the other flows within the firm: only additional revenues and costs generated by the project must be considered. If it turns out that the lifetime of some projects exceeds the budget period, the period is extended for purpose of analysis. It is essential to the traditional capital investment theory that all of the projects which will become available during the forthcoming budget period be anticipated at decision time.

With the projects enumerated and the flows determined, the worth of each project is evaluated with respect to both its net returns to the firm and the entailed risk.* Three common methods for evaluation are the payback period, the internal rate of discount, and the net present worth.[5]

With individual evaluations in hand, the preferred projects can be chosen by several techniques such as minimum rate of discount for relatively simple problems, and linear programming for more complex ones.

At first glance, this procedure for plant and equipment decisions appears applicable to deciding what markets to enter or what products to develop. In fact, some writers have extended capital investment theory to apply to the entire spectrum of business investment decisions.[6] Our objective in this chapter is to see where product-market investments differ from capital investments and what modifications in the method are needed for a practical approach to strategic decisions.

It will presently be seen that for the purpose of establishing the dimensions of the strategic problem, we shall use CIT as a 'whipping boy'. This should not be interpreted as criticism of the capital investment theory in its use for capital decisions.

STEPS IN PROBLEM SOLVING

Simon has shown[7] that solution of any decision problem in business, science, or art can be viewed in four steps.

---

* In traditional capital investment theory, the problem of risk is handled rather superficially. Much is left to the intuitive judgement of the decision maker.

1. *Perception* of decision need or opportunity. Simon calls this the *intelligence* phase.

2. *Formulation* of alternative courses of action.

3. *Evaluation* of the alternatives for their respective contributions.

4. *Choice* of one or more alternatives for implementation.

A comparison with the preceding section shows that capital investment theory is concerned with the last two steps, evaluation and choice. Perception of the need for decision and formulation of alternatives are assumed to take place prior to and outside of the framework of analysis.* As one writer puts it, 'to solve (the first two steps) there is simply no substitute for reflection. . . . There is no magic wand we can wave to produce alternatives'.[8]

1. *Perception of Need.* As suggested in Chapter 1, perception of need is a major issue in strategic decision making. A method which fails to provide for the choice between continuing concern with the operating problem as against attention to the strategic, leaves a key part of the problem to intuition and judgement. A firm, say, in the heavy chemicals industry needs a mechanism for monitoring the trends in the return on investment (which has been declining over the past ten years) and the rate of growth in demand (which has been slowing down); it needs a mechanism for recognizing whether the time has arrived to diversify. All of this should take place *before* individual diversification opportunities are sought and analysed.

Thus, CIT is incomplete for our purposes. This is a major deficiency. Our requirement is for a method which provides for continuing intelligence activity and for diagnosis of the need for strategic action.

2. *Search for Alternatives.* Traditional capital investment theory requires that all of the alternatives be known at decision time. In the strategic problem this is a rare situation. At the beginning of any planning period only a few of the alternatives will be known in sufficient detail to permit construction of cash flows. Usually, these will include the firm's traditional product-markets, current R & D projects, and perhaps some names of firms which are

---

* In fact, this feature is characteristic of a great majority of so-called management science models.

known to be interested in a merger. Other alternatives will present themselves throughout the planning period in a continual stream: product inventions in the firm's laboratories, new market opportunities, firms available for acquisition, and joint-venture opportunities. In strategic decisions such conditions of partial ignorance about future opportunities are the rule rather than the exception; a method which fails to provide for them is not addressed to a business firm.

Under conditions of partial ignorance a firm is confronted with two problems. The first is how to conduct an active search for attractive opportunities.* The second problem is to allocate the firm's limited resources among the opportunities which have been uncovered and the possibly more attractive ones which are 'just around the corner'. This is the classic 'bird in hand versus two in the bush' dilemma which is common to many decision situations in practice.

Capital investment theory is silent here, since it assumes that *all* of the decision alternatives can be enumerated and their outcomes measured. A practical method for strategic decisions must, therefore, broaden this theory by adding provisions for search and for project evaluation under partial ignorance.

3. *Project Evaluation.* CIT uses long-term profitability over the lifetime of the project as the yardstick for evaluation. Efforts to apply such a single yardstick to the strategic problem run into theoretical as well as practical difficulties.

On the conceptual level, viewpoints have been advanced by business writers and economists that profit is not the sole objective of a business firm and that a 'vector' of objectives, only one of whose components is profit, should be used.† Such a vector is usually composed of conflicting objectives; when the firm's performance is optimized on one, it is degraded on others. For example, if one of the objectives is a high degree of worker satisfaction, this can usually be attained only at the expense of profit

* To be sure, the firm can take a completely passive attitude and wait for opportunities to come to it. However, it will be shown in Chapter 6, that for most firms this leads to uncoordinated, inefficient, and potentially costly management practices.

† This viewpoint will be discussed at length in Chapter 3.

to the stockholders. CIT which uses the single yardstick is not equipped to handle either the multiplicity of objectives or the problem of conflict between them.

On the practical level it turns out that, even for the profitability component of the vector, attempts to compute cash flows for long-lived projects are frustrated by the rapid decrease in reliability of data for long-term forecasts. Since business firms are particularly interested in projects which have a long profitable life, capital investment theory turns out to be least reliable in a most important situation.

Further, on the practical level, limitations of data usually lead to cash flows which are typical of a product-market area, not ones that are specific for the opportunities in question. However, what the firm needs is not typical but *particular* flows which will reflect the unique competitive advantages of the product-market opportunity, such as superior quality, timing of product introduction, customer appeal, and competitors' reactions. While CIT implicitly requires that such effects be taken into account, it provides no method for doing so.

A related and equally important difficulty is encountered in efforts to make project projections marginal to other projects in the firm's product-market posture. This requires that cash projections take account of the joint economies and diseconomies between the project and present operations of the firm on the one hand, and between the project and all other projects under consideration on the other. As every practising manager knows, joint effects are just as difficult to reduce to pounds as uniqueness is; the task becomes prohibitive for 'breakthrough' types of product. At the same time, as we shall discuss later, proper use of joint effects and of unique characteristics are primary competitive tools in a firm which aspires to be a better-than-average business competitor. Again CIT assumes that joint effects will be taken care of *outside* the method.

REQUIREMENTS AND BACKGROUND FOR THE NEW METHOD

The preceding discussion shows that, to be applicable as a practical method for product-market decisions, capital investment

27

theory must be broadened, amended, and supplemented. It must be broadened to monitor the business environment and to search for new product-market entries under conditions of partial ignorance. It must be amended to deal with multiple conflicting objectives. It must be supplemented to identify unique product-market opportunities and joint effects. Since all of these requirements are far-reaching and fundamental, they are recorded below and will be used throughout this book as a checklist in the development of a strategic decision method. The method *must*:

1. Include all four, rather than the last two, steps of the generalized problem-solving sequence. Emphasis should be on the first two steps, monitoring the environment for changes and searching for attractive product opportunities.

2. Handle allocation of the firm's resources between opportunities in hand and probable future opportunities under conditions of partial ignorance.

3. Evaluate joint effects (synergy) resulting from addition of new product-markets to the firm.

4. Single out opportunities with outstanding competitive advantages.

5. Handle a vector of potentially antagonistic objectives.

6. Evaluate the long-term potential of projects even though cash-flow projections are unreliable.

This is an imposing list of requirements, which suggests that capital investment theory in its traditional form applies to product-market decisions only under very special conditions, i.e. when these requirements can be neglected for one reason or another. This conclusion was reached by a majority of the business community in the early days of current interest in the strategic problem of the firm. As a result, business managers began to develop practical approaches which bore little resemblance to CIT project evaluation schemes found in textbooks on economics and finance. With time these approaches found their way into business publications and thus have provided insights into the true nature of strategic business decisions.

Practical insights into 'how we did it' have been summarized in many publications, in many cases with the support of the American Management Association.[9] Among the many contributors of analytic insights into important segments of the problem are Andersen,[10] Ansoff,[11] Drucker,[12] Gilmore and Brandenburg,[13] Kline,[14] Levitt,[15] Novick,[16] Staudt,[17] Steiner,[18] Tilles,[19] and Weston.[20] A talented and prophetic Frenchman, Henri Fayol,[21] anticipated imaginatively and soundly most of the more recent analyses of modern business practice.

Recently three important books have taken a view of the business firm which is closely related to our present interest. Within a historical perspective Chandler[22] has analysed the relationship among the firm's environment, its business strategy, and its organizational structure. Sloan[23] has presented a highly illuminating history of some forty years of strategy formulation and implementation in the world's largest firm. Cyert and March[24] made a major step toward development of a theory of the firm from the decision maker's point of view.

Aside from differences of viewpoint and concepts, these three efforts complement one another, since each concerns itself with a different aspect of the total decision problem. Chandler's primary interest is in the administrative problem and its relationship to the strategic. Cyert and March concern themselves exclusively with the operating problem; their firm keeps its organization intact and its product-market posture constant. By contrast, the present book takes a comprehensive view of the strategic problem with only a minor aside to the administrative problem.

Such are the antecedents to this book in matters dealing with the nature of the firm and its function within the business environment. In the area of methodology our debt is to three primary sources. The first goes back to the results of many years of thought and study in the United States military services which have led to the development of a doctrine and methodology[25] of military decision making. The second, more recent source is the business world. As an outgrowth of concern with rapidly changing business environment, an increasing number of firms have begun to seek analytic approaches to the strategic decision making. These efforts have led to some publications on methodology.[26, 27] However, it is safe to assume that the relative newness of interest, as well as competitive considerations, have so far kept many useful methodological insights from public view.

The third source of methodological insight is the work of H. A. Simon and A. Newell.[28],[29] Although their primary interest is in human thought processes, they have developed a general methodology for problem solving which focuses on the phases of intelligence and search, thus providing a means for attacking business problems in which these two phases are also of primary importance. More recently, Reitman[30] has restated Simon's formulation in somewhat broader terms which have a direct application to the strategic decision problem.

In summary, both the conceptual foundation and tools of methodology are now at hand for an attempt at a comprehensive 'strategic decision theory of the firm', which will meet the requirements for a practical, normative method stated earlier in this section. This book represents such an attempt.

STRUCTURE OF THE NEW METHOD

As an alternative frame of reference to capital investment theory we could have used *portfolio selection theory*. While CIT deals with selection of physical assets for the firm, portfolio selection concerns selecting securities, either for an individual investor or for an investment firm.

H. Markowitz[31] has written the definitive work on portfolio selection. His work shows an even greater divergence from the strategic problem than we found to hold for CIT. However, a more recent approach taken by Clarkson[32] has many features in common with the present problem. A comparison of Clarkson's method with this book shows that our approach, when simplified for application to an investment trust, has a close similarity to Clarkson's.

Clarkson's formulation is significant to this discussion, because it sheds light on yet another requirement which is not even suggested by capital investment theory. This is the fact that, unlike CIT, the *decision rules for search and evaluation of products and markets are not the same for all firms*. In application to personal investment policies Clarkson shows that a person's profession, adequacy of current earnings, tax bracket, and legal restrictions on estate all affect the choice of the preferred portfolio of securities. This preference will naturally undergo changes as the above conditions change in the course of the investor's life. Similarly, the decision rules for product-market selection vary from firm to firm and, within a firm, from one time period to another. This is a direct consequence of requirements 1 and 5 listed in the preceding section.

Since objectives are no longer a simple yardstick, they will vary from one type of firm to another depending on the firm's past profitability, its prospects, and its stage in the life cycle. For example, an infant firm trying to gain a toehold will focus attention on current profitability, whereas a large firm entrenched in the market-place will turn attention to long-term growth prospects. Since a firm has to search for opportunities, it will also tend to adapt search rules to the particular opportunities which confront it. Thus a firm with large fixed investments will narrow its search to opportunities to which this investment can be applied, while a firm with highly liquid assets may range wide in search of new product-markets.

The fact that decision rules vary is the foundation for our approach to the problem. Our concern must be not only with *evaluation* of projects for given rules, which is the main concern of CIT, but also with *formulation* of the rules for each individual firm. Further, the focus of interest is on the formulation aspect. While project evaluation is quite similar to CIT, formulation of decision rules requires a novel approach. Formulation of rules plays a determining role in the overall process because, as Simon has shown,[33] it tends to predetermine the final choice of the individual product-markets. It is clear, for example, that if a firm decides to confine search to its traditional industry, this decision will heavily predetermine the future pattern of profitability even before individual products and markets are identified.

We shall deal with the strategic problems on two levels and in two steps. On the first level we shall consider the characteristics of the firm's total position, to derive decision rules for search and evaluation of opportunities. Drucker and Levitt[34] have aptly characterized this step as deciding what kind of business the firm is in and what kind of business it should be in. Two decision rules in their totality describe this concept. One, which sets the

31

yardsticks for the firm's performance, deals with the objectives of the firm. The other, which defines the desirable characteristics of products and markets, deals with the product-market *strategy*. The two sets of rules have a means-ends relationship; objectives set the goals, and strategy sets the path to the goals.

On the second level the rules are applied to individual opportunities whenever they occur and however they come about. Here the approach is somewhat similar to CIT. The differences are in 1. application of strategy to screen the opportunities, 2. use of a vector of objectives, and 3. use of additional qualitative yardsticks to refine measurement of profitability.

OUTLINE OF THE ADAPTIVE SEARCH METHOD FOR STRATEGY FORMULATION

As the title indicates, the method uses a search procedure in arriving at a strategy. This is accomplished through a 'cascade' approach: at the outset possible decision rules are formulated in gross terms and are then successively refined through several stages as the solution proceeds. This gives the appearance of solving the problem several times over, but with successively more precise results. The first step is to decide between the two major alternatives: to diversify or not to diversify the firm. The second step is to choose a broad product-market scope for the firm from a list of broad industrial categories. The third is to refine the scope in terms of characteristics or product-markets within it.*

For example, a firm in the basic chemicals industry may analyse its past performance and prospects and arrive at a decision to seek diversification. As the second step it would decide that a closely related industry is the natural direction to follow and pick fertilizers as its preferred area. This would be followed by a detailed analysis of the firm in relation to the competitive characteristics of fertilizer firms. The end product would be

* This approach of successive convergence on the solution should be contrasted with the more usual method in management science in which an effort is made at the first stage to enumerate all of the final alternatives and then to construct an evaluation scheme to compare them.

specific decision rules such as the competitive and joint effect interactions desired for the new product entry. Thus armed with a concept of the business it wishes to become, the firm would begin to seek out, create, and evaluate opportunities.

Another important characteristic of this process is feedback. Since the cascade is a process of search for the best solution, information may develop at later stages which casts doubt on previous decisions.

Thus the chemical firm may discover that it does not have as good a match with the fertilizer business as appeared on preliminary rough examination. It will then re-examine the previous choice of the product-market scope.

The procedure within each step of the cascade is similar. 1. A set of objectives is established. 2. The difference (the 'gap') between the current position of the firm and the objectives is estimated. 3. One or more courses of action (strategy) is proposed. 4. These are tested for their 'gap-reducing properties'. A course is accepted if it substantially closes the gap; if it does not, new alternatives are tried.*

To continue our simple example, the chemical firm may choose 12 per cent annual rate of return on investment (ROI) as its sole objective (this is highly unlikely in real life, but helps the example; see Chapter 3). It finds that past history and current trends show that 8 per cent ROI is the best that can be attained with maximum effort in the chemical business. The gap is 4 per cent. Trends in the fertilizer industry indicate an average 14 per cent return for the industry. To attain a 12 per cent average, a certain size of acquisition is needed. A test is made to see whether an acquisition of such size within a reasonable period of time is within the firm's resources. If the answer is yes, the fertilizer industry is selected; but the result is provisional, because later stages of analysis may show that the chemical firm's chances of doing *as well* as the average in the fertilizer industry are not very great, or that a

* Again a comparison with more usual management science approaches shows a difference. In the adaptive search method the firm is 'satisfizing' rather than 'optimizing' its behaviour. Hence no assurance is obtained that the decision rules selected represent in any sense 'the best of all possible choices'.

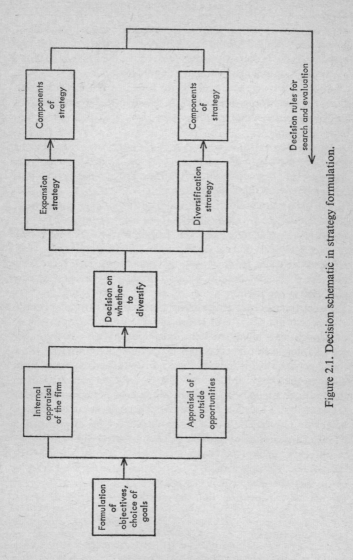

Figure 2.1. Decision schematic in strategy formulation.

much larger investment will be needed than was originally anticipated.*

The example points to another feature of the method which introduces the word 'adaptive' into the title.

Suppose that the firm cannot find any industry through which it can attain a 12 per cent ROI. In that case the goal will have to be revised downward. Or a more happy event, suppose the fertilizer entry looks so promising that even 15 per cent would be reasonable. Up goes the goal.

Thus the method has what Reitman[35] calls 'open constraint' property; both the objectives and the evaluation of the present position are subject to revision as a result of insights obtained in the process of solution.

To summarize briefly, the adaptive search method was described above in its application to formulation of a product-market strategy for a business firm. Its salient characteristics are 1. a 'cascade' procedure of successive narrowing and refining the decision rules, 2. feed-back between stages in the cascade, 3. a gap-reduction process within each stage, and 4. adaptation of both objectives and starting-point evaluation.†

The concepts of strategy and of objectives are the keys to successful application of the method. Therefore, the next few chapters will explore how product-market decisions relate to these concepts in practice. Then, a decision flow diagram will be constructed which applies the adaptive search method to the problem in hand. Although somewhat prematurely, we would like to give the reader a simplified schematic of this diagram as a means for relating various chapters to the final product. This schematic is shown in Figure 2.1, where for simplicity all feed-back relations have been omitted.

---

* The pristine beauty of this example should not deceive the reader, it is merely illustrative. Many were the times when the author wished that strategic problems were this clear cut and simple.

† For more detailed discussion of methodology see Refs. 36 to 40.

CHAPTER 3
Objectives

... with regard to an individual enterprise, the question of profit is of great importance as an economic indicator of its efficiency.

NIKITA KHRUSHCHEV

We, as business people, can fulfil our obligation to society in the everyday process of running our businesses. . . . Businessmen should be proud of the contribution they are making . . . not apologetic because they are making money.

MEYER KESTENBAUM

THE PROBLEM

IN Chapter 1 we described a business firm as a *purposive* organization whose behaviour is directed toward identifiable end purposes or objectives. When made explicit within the firm, objectives become tools of many uses in appraisal of performance, control, coordination, as well as all phases of the decision process. Their potential pervasiveness is such that objectives have been used as a basis for an integrated view on the entire management process which has become known as 'management by objectives'.[41] Our interest in this book is in only one of these uses, namely, the role which objectives play in strategic decisions. This means that we shall be concerned with objectives of the firm as a whole and shall not deal with the very important problem of the organizational hierarchy of objectives which are essential to the operating problem of the firm.[42] Nor shall we be concerned with the process by which objectives are derived, whether they are imposed from above by top management, generated through a synthesis of lower-level objectives, or arrived at through a bargaining process among participants in the firm. We shall, however, be concerned with the business, economic, and social variables which determine the objectives, regardless of the process by which they are formulated.

The central question, which must be resolved before specific values are assigned, is what kind of objectives should the firm seek: maximum profit, maximum value of stockholders' equity, or a balanced satisfaction of its 'stockholders'.

One way to an answer is through philosophy – a study of ethical, aesthetic, and economic values within the firm and the socioeconomic-political environment. The answer, hopefully, would be a statement of what the firm's role and objectives *should* be in modern society. Several philosophically different approaches will be discussed below; while each has apparent merit, none appears to have a clear advantage over the others.

Another way to the answer is through a historical analysis of business objectives that have been used and how they have evolved. Since explicit use of objectives is a relatively recent management technique, this approach is difficult. Little appears to have been done in this direction except a survey of current practice.[43]

A third approach is to construct a system of objectives which is consistent and usable on one hand, and which can be related to current business practice on the other. This is the approach we shall use in this chapter. Starting with an assumption that long-term profitability is the central objective in the firm, we shall construct a system of objectives which can be individually related to performance yardsticks commonly used in business practice.

As the first step, this chapter is devoted to laying foundations. Several currently popular philosophies of objectives will be described and compared, a new philosophy will be formulated, and the central business objective will be described. The next chapter will take up the task of converting this theoretical formulation into a usable system of objectives.

CURRENT PHILOSOPHIES

At first glance, the question of the objectives of a business firm would appear to be non-controversial. Traditionally and historically, a business firm has been regarded as an economic institution; it has developed a measurement of efficiency – profit – which is common and unique to business. It would seem, therefore, that profit-seeking, or maximization of profit, would be the natural single business objective. In actual fact, objectives are currently one of the most controversial issues of business ethics. Distinguished writers have sought to remove profit from its position

37

as the central motive in business and replace it with doctrines such as equal responsibility to stockholders, long-term survival, or a negotiated consensus among various participants in the firm. Some have branded profit as immoral and socially unacceptable.[44] The situation is confused to the point where Mr Khrushchev proclaims the importance of profit, while a distinguished American business leader feels compelled to defend the role of profit in American society.[45] Several reasons can be advanced for this confused state of affairs.

The first is the growing conflict between long- and short-term demands for the firm's resources. During the eighteenth and nineteenth centuries, before technology made necessary long-term product research and long-term anticipation of capital-equipment needs, it seemed appropriate to use short-term profitability as a yardstick of the firm's success. Increasingly in the twentieth century, and more rapidly after World War II, the influx of technology and increasing capital-equipment needs have forced concern with long-term problems. And yet, if short-term profitability were to remain the principal performance yardstick, investments in projects with long-term maturity would naturally be neglected. The result would be a threat to the very survival of the firm in the long run. To assure survival, the concept of the firm's objectives must be expanded to cover the long-term horizon.

The microeconomic theory of the firm – a major body of theory which gave rise to the nineteenth-century concept of profit maximization – could not accommodate this expansion for two reasons. First, because it is basically a steady-state theory concerned with successive equilibrium conditions and thus not capable of dealing with distinctions between short- and long-range horizons; and, secondly, because it does not recognize the exchange between investments for current profit and those for future returns.[46]

In recent years a number of economists and business writers have offered alternatives to short-term profit maximization such as maximization of the company's net present worth,[47] maximization of market value of the firm,[48] or profit-constrained maximization of growth.[49] Each of these, taken by itself, is logically persuasive, but none appears superior on philosophical grounds nor conclusively supported by data derived from experience.

A sharp break with the profit maximization tradition was made by Drucker, who proposed survival as the central purpose of the firm. This is to be accomplished through pursuit of a set of 'survival objectives' based on five 'survival functions' which the firm must fulfil to stay alive. Although 'adequate' profitability is among the objectives, according to Drucker, ' "profit maximization" is the wrong concept whether it be interpreted to mean short-range or long-range profits'.[50]

The problems resulting from the deficiencies of the historical short-term profit maximization concept are by no means resolved. They are further compounded by the growing importance of the firm as a social institution.

In reaction to the public outrages at the 'smash'n-grab imperialism' of the nineteenth century, business has acquired a sense of social responsibility to society in general and participants in the firm in particular. Thus Frank Abrams speaks of the firm's responsibility to 'maintain an equitable and working balance among the claims of the various directly interested groups – stockholders, employees, customers, and the public at large'.[51]

While, as we shall see later, 'responsibilities' and 'objectives' are not synonymous, they have been made one in a 'stakeholder theory' of objectives. This theory maintains that the objectives of the firm should be derived by balancing the conflicting claims of the various 'stakeholders' in the firm: managers, workers, stockholders, suppliers, vendors. The firm has a responsibility to all of these and must configure its objectives so as to give each a measure of satisfaction. Profit which is a return on the investment to the stockholders is one of such satisfactions, but does not necessarily receive special predominance in the objective structure.[52]

The philosophy of objectives has been further complicated by structural changes within the firm. One such change has been a major shift from ownership by a few individuals to ownership by many small shareholders. It created professional management cadres, working for a salary, virtually in control of the firm's fortunes, and guided by personal ambitions of their own. The objectives of top management can and frequently do come in conflict

with objectives of other stakeholders in the firm and in particular with those of the equity owners. Thus, the desire of a chairman to remain in control of a firm until his retirement age would
lead him late in his career to become a cautious and conservative
decision maker. At that very time the firm's long-term survival
may well depend on radical strategic changes such as abandoning
the traditional line of business and diversifying. Faced with the
conflict between his own security and the firm's welfare, the president presumably would avoid leading the firm into such change
and would, instead, assure other managers, stockholders, and the
board that there is no need to rock the boat, that the problem is
really not that serious.

Some writers who raise this problem of the management-
owner conflict cite other important examples but propose no
constructive solutions for guiding the firm's behaviour. Others
argue that the conflict is more apparent than real and that professional interests and ethics of the manager are, in the last analysis, consonant with the maximum profitability concept.[53]

Another structural change in the firm has been growth in size
and complexity. The resulting philosophy of decentralized profit
and loss responsibility, which in America culminated in the 1920s
in the doctrine of centralized policy-making with decentralized
operations control, has led to a wide delegation of decision-
making power in the firm.[54] Thus the decision process now consists of many local decisions which are based on local limited
information and are in potential conflict with one another. Some-
how these add up to consensus decisions on central issues of the
firm. This change has dealt a severe blow not only to the economist's concept of profit maximization but also to the validity of
the microeconomic theory in explaining behaviour of the firm. A
'managerialist' point of view came into being which, in a substantial body of writings, subjected the microeconomic theory to
thorough criticism. While the managerialists have offered a number of substitute explanations of the behaviour of the firm, until
recently none has produced a practical guide to business decisions.[55] Now substantial progress toward this end has been made
by Cyert and March in *A Behavioral Theory of the Firm*.[56] In
consonance with the managerialist outlook, they argue that

'organizations do not have objectives, only people have objectives'. Therefore, the objectives of a firm are in reality a negotiated consensus of objectives of the influential participants. This has the ring of the stakeholder theory, except that in the former the resolution of conflicting claims is presumably made by a benevolent judicious agency (top management?), whereas Cyert and March suggest that the consensus is negotiated by the participants and is renegotiated as it becomes unstable because of changes in power position or in outside business conditions.

The great value of the Cyert and March theory lies in the fact that it offers for the first time a common framework for the economic and the managerialist points of view by admitting both economic and social variables into the decision-making process. Unfortunately, the present state of development of their theory falls short of the requirements of the strategic problem. For one thing their approach describes how *some* firms' objective formation processes take place. These happen to be the very types of firms which either refuse to make, or do not have to make, strategic decisions. Therefore, the discussion is limited to the operating rather than the strategic problem of the firm. For another thing, while Cyert and March have described the general characteristics of the negotiation process which takes place in forming objectives, they have not yet succeeded in showing how specific objectives evolve within the firm.

BASIS FOR A PRACTICAL SYSTEM OF OBJECTIVES

The preceding survey leaves the subject in a rather unsatisfactory state. If one were interested in the objectives as a detached observer, the variety of opinions would offer much material for further comparison and speculation. Since our specific interest is in objectives as tools for management, choices and commitments must be made from a particular point of view. Thus it is clear that the choice of philosophy will have to be made by each firm for itself. The management responsible – the board, the corporate management, and the key operating managers – will have to arrive at a consensus within the present power structure of the firm.

However, once this is done, it will be found that most of the conflicting systems of objectives have not been related by their proponents to the system of performance measurements which currently exists within business firms. In fact, some formulations have not been specific enough to permit a determination of whether such a relation exists.* If it turns out that a particular system of objectives will require a brand-new way of collecting, processing, and presenting business data, the cost of instituting such a system would be formidable. Further, the firm would find itself operating on a double standard: one the traditional accounting approach to measurement of performance, and the other the new data system designed to tell the firm whether objectives are being met.

Clearly, this is a very unsatisfactory solution, which should be avoided if possible. Objectives need to be made compatible with the existing information-processing systems within the firm. In order to meet this requirement we shall develop in this and the following chapter a system of objectives which is based on the following premises.

1. The firm has both (a) 'economic' objectives aimed at optimizing the efficiency of its total resource-conversion process and (b) 'social' or non-economic objectives, which are the result of interaction among individual objectives of the firm's participants.

2. In most firms the economic objectives exert the primary influence on the firm's behaviour and form the main body of explicit goals used by management for guidance and control of the firm.

3. The central purpose of the firm is to maximize long-term return on resources employed within the firm.

4. The social objectives exert a secondary modifying and constraining influence on management behaviour.

5. In addition to proper objectives two related types of influence are exerted on management behaviour: responsibilities and constraints.[58]

* This is not to say that some could not be developed to this point. For example, Drucker's system of objectives could be developed to make uses of current management information.[57]

a. Objectives are decision rules which enable management to guide and measure the firm's performance toward its purpose.

b. Responsibilities are obligations which the firm undertakes to discharge. They do not form a part of the firm's internal guidance and control mechanism. For example, the responsibility for the support of the Ford Foundation does not affect in any way the Ford Company's decisions about how to sell automobiles, what types of new models to develop, what new markets to invade, or the choice of non-automotive diversification moves.

c. Constraints are decision rules which exclude certain options from the firm's freedom actions. For example, the minimum wage level is usually a legal or contractual constraint, not an objective, unless the firm consciously chooses to raise it either above the legal minimum or above the level negotiated with the union.

In the perspective of the discussion in the preceding section our basic philosophy can be viewed as an attempt to reconcile several of the points of view. The benefit of the doubt is given clearly to the 'traditionalist' approach of the economist, but with the addition of a long-term view of profitability. At the same time, the 'managerial' influence is admitted as a modifier to the final system of objectives.

Our approach is not necessarily more rigorous or conceptually attractive than several of the approaches discussed earlier. We do have in our favour the fact that our method is related to experience. As will be shown in the next chapter, we have the benefit of a clear relationship between objectives and common business performance measurements. Thus the approach has merit to the extent to which current practice is *good* practice.

BASIC ECONOMIC OBJECTIVE

Contrary to the assumption of Cyert and March, we assume that the business firm does have objectives which are different and distinct from individual objectives of the participants. This does not say that the latter are not important and influential in modifying the former, but it does say that objectives for an institution known as a business firm can be inferred from its relationship to the environment, from its internal structure, from the functions it

43

performs, and from its past history. This does not lead to the conclusion that objectives of all firms are identical, but rather, as we shall see, to a conclusion that they are drawn from the same master list.

Our second major assumption is that the firm seeks to optimize the efficiency of its resource-conversion process. The return to the firm, or profit, is optimized in some sense in relation to the resources employed to produce it.

To make this concept meaningful, we need the idea of the *time horizon* of a firm – the period over which the firm seeks to optimize its resource-conversion efficiency. Most large publicly held corporations are legally and practically assumed to exist in perpetuity, i.e. their time horizon is infinite. There are many cases of smaller and closely held firms where the time horizon is finite. For example, owners of a small electronics firm, who seek to build the firm up to a point at which it can be sold under attractive capital gains terms, would view time horizon as terminating at the time of the sale or merger, since new resources, management, and perspective would come into play at that time.

We define an *objective* as a measure of efficiency of the resource-conversion process. An objective contains three elements: the particular *attribute* that is chosen as a measure of efficiency, the *yardstick*, or scale, by which the attribute is measured, and the *goal* – the particular value on the scale which the firm seeks to attain.

We have selected return on the firm's equity as the attribute* and the average rate of returns on equity over the time horizon as the yardstick for the overall objective of the firm. The goal is to optimize this return. To put this in more concise terms, the primary economic objective is to optimize the long-term rate of return on the equity employed in the firm.

The key idea is selecting *profitability* (a measure of return on

* Business literature has reflected a lively controversy over whether the owners' equity or total assets, or working capital plus fixed assets is the appropriate denominator for ROI computations. Our view is that equity provides an all-inclusive measure of top management's performance, including skill in use of outside financing. On the other hand, the other denominators may be appropriate for appraisal of performance on management levels charged primarily with *operating* responsibilities.

resources) rather than *profit* (excess of revenues over cost) for the principal attribute. In economic theory the maximum profit is reached at a level of sales at which incremental costs of goods just balance the incremental revenues. The implied assumption is that the resources employed in the firm can be adjusted at will and scaled down or up to the exact amount needed to sustain the optimum level of sales. In practice the resources in a firm are not flexible, and a change in equity base is always associated with tangible costs to the firm. Expansion of equity entails underwriting fees plus other less tangible but frequently important costs due to changes in the pattern of ownership. Contraction of equity base is more costly, since it usually involves liquidation of fixed assets at a considerable discount from their original cost to the firm. Further, the process of equity liquidation is time-consuming and could not be carried out without serious effect on market evaluation of the firm by the investing public. In summary, the problem of the firm in practice is how to make available resources yield the best possible return, rather than to maximize profit on the assumption that the resources base can be adjusted at will.

The second distinctive point in our formulation of objectives is selection of the rate of return on the investment as the yardstick of profitability. We could have chosen others; Solomon, for example, chooses the *difference* between net present value of revenues and present value of investment.[59] There is no absolutely 'correct' yardstick – each has its advantages and dangers.* Our choice is suggested by the following reasons: 1. Rate of return on investment is a common and widely accepted yardstick for measuring business success. 2. Unlike other formulations, it permits us to sidestep the presently unresolved problem of what constitutes the appropriate rate of discount for future uses of capital.† 3. Rate of return is a common and convenient yardstick for comparison of business prospects in different industries.

* For example, unthinking use of a ratio for profitability measurements can lead to the unrealistic conclusion that the best way to maximize performance is to reduce equity to zero, which will make the return theoretically infinite!

† Mathematically inclined readers will easily see that the average of ratios of return by period is equivalent to the average of ratios of present values of return to the present values of investment taken by period.

Thus far, while our objective is realistic and is measured by a commonly used business ratio, we are, unfortunately, very far from a usable objective. We specified the time horizon of the firm as the period over which profitability is to be measured, and recognized at the same time that for most firms the horizon is infinite! We require that profitability be maximized, and yet in Chapter 2 a big point was made of the fact that many of the alternatives the firm will encounter are not known at decision time.[60] The next task, therefore, is to tackle these problems. In the process we shall make progress in meeting requirements 2. and 6. set forth in Chapter 2.

CHAPTER 4

A Practical System of Objectives

Long-Range Goals:
    1. Health – more leisure.
    2. Money.
    3. Write book (play?) – fame////??
    4. Visit India.
Immediate:
    Pick up pattern at Hilda's.
    Change faucets – call plumber (who?).
    Try yoghurt??

FROM THE DIARY OF A LADY QUOTED IN
THE *New Yorker*

THE PROBLEM

WE shall approach practical objectives through a series of approximations. Keeping the maximization of the rate of return as the central theoretical objective, we shall develop a number of subsidiary objectives (which the economists call *proxy* variables) which contribute in different ways to improvement in the return and which are also measurable in business practice. A firm which meets high performance in most of its subsidiary objectives will substantially enhance its long-term rate of return.* As will be seen, this road has its own obstacles: the difficulties of long-term maximization are replaced by the problem of reconciling claims of conflicting objectives.

PROXIMATE OBJECTIVE AND PARTIAL IGNORANCE

The first step is to deal with the problem of the time horizon. For most firms this will be very distant, theoretically at infinity. In contrast, the period for which reasonably reliable profitability forecasts can be constructed is relatively short and varies between three and ten years. When taken beyond five years, most profit

---

* The defect in our approach is that we cannot prove that the result will be a 'maximum' possible overall return.

forecasts become unreliable because of a great many uncertainties in the future state of technology, the company's share of the market, future management skills, general economic climate, and political climate.

We shall refer to the period for which the firm is able to construct forecasts with an accuracy of, say, plus or minus 20 per cent as the *planning horizon* of the firm. This divides the firm's time horizon into two parts: what we shall call the *proximate period* (three to ten years) which extends to the planning horizon, and the *long-term* period from the planning to the time horizon. The latter may be very long indeed.

Within the proximate period, data are adequate for direct measurement of return on investment. There is no need, therefore, for proxy objectives. Values of ROI can be selected as reference goals and thenceforth used for evaluation of different product-market entries. The question of relative risk of different opportunities is of great importance. Since ROI is what is usually called an expected value measure (it uses probable values of contributing variables) it does not discriminate between risky opportunities and less risky ones. Unfortunately, theory has produced very few useful insights for dealing with risk. In most formulations the final exchange between prospective gain (ROI) and the risk is left to the decision maker. Therefore, for practical purposes we suggest that, following customary practice, the firm establish three levels for ROI, each adjusted to the relative riskiness of opportunities. The reference level is the value of the ROI which will be determined as *the* proximate objective by methods which will be presently discussed. This level will be applied to a majority of opportunities which are judged to be 'normally' risky. A high level of desired ROI is then set up for opportunities which are judged to be very risky, and a correspondingly low level of acceptable profitability for opportunities which are a near 'sure thing'.*

The next issue is how to select the reference level for ROI. If all

* For example, some firms require that the expected rate of return on very risky projects be twice that for normal projects. Thus a firm which requires 15 per cent after tax ROI from most projects, may, on occasion, reject opportunities which promise as much as 20 to 25 per cent.

opportunities which will lay claim to the firm's resources during the forthcoming budget period could be anticipated in advance, the conventional procedure of capital investment theory could be used. First, tentative values for ROI would be selected for each class and opportunities in each class arranged in order of their ROI prospects. If resources available to the firm were used up by opportunities above the minimum required ROI levels a subset with a preferred mix of risks would be chosen. If too few opportunities qualified, minimum required values might be adjusted downward, or only the qualifying opportunities chosen.

As discussed before, in most real-world situations only some of the alternatives are known at the beginning of the budget period. Others are only dimly perceived. How should a firm go about establishing realistic ROI levels so that it does not end up regretting early overcommitment of resources on the one hand, or having been overly 'stingy' on the other? Peter Drucker has diagnosed the problem in more general terms as follows: 'We cannot rest content with developing plans for the events which we either foresee or want to foresee. We must prepare for all possible and a good many impossible contingencies. We must have a workable solution or at least the approach to it – for anything that may come up.'[61]

The resolution of this 'bird in hand versus two in the bush' dilemma is helped by the fact that, as was indicated earlier, the ignorance about future opportunities is not total but partial. While many individual products, customers, or company acquisitions cannot be specified in advance, the characteristics of the industries in which these will occur, the probability of their occurrence, and their general characteristics can. For example, a firm interested in entering the electronics industry may not be able to specify in advance the individual products and markets it will have two years hence. It can, however, diagnose the particular kind of technology which will characterize the product line, the overall growth prospects, the nature of the competition, the typical patterns of return on sales, return on investment, and price/earnings ratios. Thus, in reality the condition is one of partial, rather than total, ignorance.* If the firm raises its sights

* Condition of partial ignorance is different from the types of situations

from individual products to groups of product-markets, much information is available for decision making.

One way to use this information is first to estimate the average expected ROI for industries in which the firm is interested and also the ROI for outstanding and for below-average opportunities. For an existing industry this can be approximated by analysing past and present performance of firms in the industry ranging from poor to outstanding. For a product-market entry which is the start of a brand-new industry the task is much more difficult and must be undertaken through historical comparison to similar industries. In both cases past and present performance is extrapolated into the future with the aid of knowledge about economic trends and trends in the product-market demand for the industry.

Next, a *range* of values of ROI is selected for the reference risk class. The value at the high end of the range represents a highly desirable *goal*, the value at the low end the acceptance *threshold* below which opportunities are not accepted. The goal-threshold values are based on the following factors:

1. Past, present, and future ROI characteristics of the industries in which the firm is interested, including the average and the spread, as described above.

2. An estimate of the number of opportunities which the firm may encounter during the next budget period. For company acquisition programmes this would be derived from a count of firms in the industry which are of appropriate size and an assessment of the intensity of diversification activity. For internal product development this would be based on an assessment of the probable output from research and development.

3. The urgency of strategic action by the firm during the forthcoming budget period. If the profitability picture urgently needs a near-term boost, a more modest goal and a lower threshold will be acceptable than would be in a case when the strategic action is taken for its long-term contribution.

---

treated in the bulk of mathematical theory for decisions under risk and uncertainty. In the latter all of the specific decision alternatives are assumed known. The uncertainty and risk are ascribed in various degrees to the likelihood of their occurrence, or their outcome.

4. The amount of resource (or the size of the entry) which the firm wants to commit to product-market changes during the budget period. Again, if the firm's ambitions are modest, a high goal and a narrow range are indicated. If much money is to be spent, the firm should be prepared to be less choosy.

The goal-threshold range thus established becomes the proximate yardstick for evaluation of opportunities. Those below threshold are rejected, those above are evaluated as being more or less desirable depending on how close they are to the goal. The usefulness of the range of values lies in the fact that it permits relative ratings, even when a single opportunity is being looked at. This would not be possible if the problem were approached through setting only one reference value, either the threshold, or the goal.*

The approach to the partial-ignorance problem described above can thus be seen to take advantage of usually available knowledge of industry characteristics, even when individual opportunities in the industry cannot be anticipated. It presents a very general technique which can be applied to other objectives and to elements of strategy. *Unless otherwise specified, we shall assume that all other decision rules discussed in the book will be expressed in the form of threshold goals.*

Attention should be called to the significant aspect of the adaptive search method which is illustrated above and which will recur repeatedly through the book. This is the circular dependence of the goals on the environment and of the choice of environment on the goals. While the management at the outset will have some ideas about the value of proximate ROI it wishes to achieve, before the final values are selected it will have to modify the original aspirations in the light of the firm's capabilities and of available opportunities. This illustrates what is meant by the 'open-ended constraint' property of the strategic problem.

* In this respect our approach appears to us to be superior to a single level 'aspiration level' approach advocated by H. Simon, W. Morris, and others. On the other hand our approach can be shown to be a 'poor man's' practical variant for a mathematical formulation of the same problem which has been offered by Kaufman.[62]

LONG-TERM OBJECTIVES

Exclusive concern with proximate profitability would be almost certain to leave the firm run down at the end of the period. Total emphasis would be on current products and markets: on advertising, promotion, sales force, productivity of the manufacturing organization. But to remain profitable into the long term, the firm must continue to renew itself; new resources must be brought in and new products and markets must be developed. Many key phases of this self-renewal activity have long lead times. Therefore, during the proximate period resource commitments must be made to such long-term needs as research and development, management training, and new plant and equipment.

If the behaviour of the firm were guided solely by the proximate objective, expenditures for such purposes could not be justified and would be given very low priorities. It is essential, therefore, to establish long-term objectives aimed at maintaining and increasing profitability after the proximate period. The obstacle to setting these is that accurate ROI forecasts and measurements cannot be made for the long-term period.

A way around this obstacle is to abandon efforts to measure long-term profitability directly and to measure, instead, characteristics of the firm which contribute to it. One major category of these is concerned with continued improvement of the external competitive position.

1. Continuing growth of sales *at least* at the pace of the industry to enable the firm to maintain its share of the market.

2. Increase in relative market share to increase relative efficiency of the firm.

3. Growth in earnings to provide resources for reinvestment.

4. Growth in earnings per share to attract new capital to the firm.

5. Continuing addition of new products and product lines.

6. Continuing expansion of the firm's customer population.

7. Absence of excessive seasonal or cyclical fluctuations in sales and earnings and of consequent loss of competitive position

through externally forced inefficiency in the use of the firm's resources.

Each of these factors is a partial indicator of long-term profitability potential; taken together they assure that the firm will have a strong competitive position vis-à-vis the environment.

To make good on this position, internal efficiency must be maintained. An overall, but not necessarily reliable, indicator is the trend in earnings per share. It is unreliable because behind it may lurk a failure to invest in long-term growth such as would occur, for example, if the firm failed to modernize plant or maintain long-lead time inventories. Therefore, more direct indicators of efficiency are needed.

1. If turnover ratios are comparable to or better than those of competition, indications are strong that the firm is making good use of its resources. A key turnover ratio is return on sales; supporting ones are turnover of working capital, net worth, inventory, etc. Another key ratio is debt/equity, which indicates how well the firm uses its borrowing capacity.

2. Depth of critical skills is a key indicator of future profitability. This may be measured by depth of management, of skilled personnel, and of research and development talent.

3. Human and organizational assets must be backed up by modern physical assets. Among yardsticks are the age of plant, machinery, and inventory.

These *proxy* (lower-level) yardsticks form a hierarchy which relates to the overall long-term objective of the firm in the manner shown in Figure 4.1. The hierarchy shown has no organizational implications, since our interest is primarily in relating internal proxy measurements to overall profitability of the firm.

The structure of Figure 4.1 suggests an answer to a question which is frequently asked: If ROI is the ultimate measure of the firm's performance, why should management be concerned with the variety of contributing proxy measurements? The answer is that, *theoretically* long-term ROI does indeed subsume other variables, but since in *practice* ROI can only be reliably computed over the proximate period, the other goals must be brought in as a measure of long-term dynamics of the firm.

Proxy measurements below the level of ROI are also essential

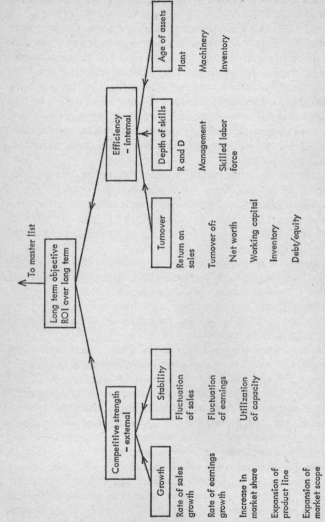

Figure 4.1. Hierarchy of the long term objective.

for diagnostic analysis of the firm's performance. For example, poor profitability may be traced to incomplete utilization of plant, to the inherent inefficiency of obsolete plant, or to an increase in selling expense out of proportion to the growth in sales. A systematic diagnostic procedure for such analysis has been developed in the so-called 'Du Pont system' of financial control.[63]

The proxy measurements shown in Figure 4.1 have been selected to make use of data which are commonly generated for such diagnostic purposes. This is why Figure 4.1 shows many familiar financial ratios. This overlap is highly desirable, because it avoids the necessity of creating a new system of measurement within the firm.

However, the overlap should not obscure the basically different ultimate uses of information. Traditionally it has been used for diagnosis and trend analysis. We propose that the common yardsticks be put to further uses: setting objectives, evaluating the firm's position against these objectives, and evaluating prospective product-market entries.

Selection-reference values for this purpose is similar to setting proximate objectives. For a majority of yardsticks shown in Figure 4.1 quantitative goal-threshold values can be set. For a few others qualitative statements are made such as 'acquire basic research competence in very low temperature physics'.

These goals are then applied to respective opportunities as they occur. Not all of the proxy yardsticks will be applicable to all opportunities. Thus when acquisition of a substantial company is considered, the entire gamut of variables which contribute to long-term profitability will probably be relevant. On the other hand, small acquisitions, acquisitions of products, or internal product developments usually contribute mostly to the competitive strength and may offer little for improvement in efficiency. In this case the block of variables on the right-hand side of Figure 4.1 would be largely irrelevant to the evaluation.

FLEXIBILITY OBJECTIVE – ANOTHER ASPECT
OF PARTIAL IGNORANCE

Proximate and long-term objectives evaluate product-market opportunities in the light of the probable trends in the industry and the economy. However, the probable trends can be upset by unforeseeable events which may have relatively low probability of occurrence, but whose impact on profitability of the opportunity and on the firm as a whole would be major. The impact may be negative, with catastrophic consequences, or positive (the word 'breakthrough' is often used to describe it), opening wide vistas to the firm. An example of a catastrophic event might even be an act of God, such as an early frost in Florida; an economic depression; or a drastic political change, such as a revolution in a South American country in which the firm has major investments. On the more immediate level, catastrophe might be a decision by a single customer, to whom a firm has been selling its entire output for many years, to take his trade elsewhere. Invention of the transistor was a breakthrough for many companies and a catastrophe for others. Acquisition of electrostatic printing patents was certainly a breakthrough for Xerox; so was Land's invention of a new photographic press.

Although some catastrophes can be anticipated, a firm which tries to predict revolutions and inventions is undertaking a highly unproductive job. On the other hand, a firm can effectively buy insurance against catastrophes and put itself in the way of potential discoveries. This can be done by adding another major objective to the firm's master list – a *flexibility objective*. Flexibility can be measured by two proxy objectives: *external* flexibility achieved through a diversified pattern of product-market investments, and *internal* flexibility through liquidity of resources.

External flexibility is best described by the maxim of not putting all of one's eggs in a single basket. This is achieved through a product-market posture which is sufficiently diversified to minimize the effect of a catastrophe and/or to put the firm into areas in which it can benefit from likely breakthroughs. Thus external flexibility can be either defensive, aggressive, or both. A classic example of the search for defensive flexibility has been the desire of many aircraft–missile companies for a fifty-fifty split between government and civilian business. The failure by most such companies to achieve this indicates the difficulty of attaining flexibility.

Defensive flexibility can be measured in several ways:

1. By the number of independent * customers which take a substantial portion of the firm's sales. The single-customer defence industry firm, or a 'captive' supplier to Sears are examples of firms with the least flexibility.

2. By the number of market segments in the firm's posture which belong to different economies. Thus a firm which sells refrigerators in the United States, the Common Market, and Japan has a higher flexibility than a solely domestic supplier.

3. By the number of independent technologies underlying the firm's product-market posture. Thus a firm in electronics, biochemistry, and molecular optics would have a high degree of flexibility.

Aggressive flexibility is more elusive and harder to implement and measure. Instead of minimizing the shock of catastrophes, it maximizes the chance of participating in breakthroughs.

1. One measure is the firm's participation in areas of technology which are in ferment. Although not subject to quantitative measurement, these can be singled out by perceptive management with the aid of competent technical advice. Examples of areas which currently appear to be in ferment and fraught with breakthrough prospects are molecular optics, bionics, and oceanography.

2. Another essential measure is the relative strength of the firm's research and development in these areas. Even if the firm does not make the actual breakthrough, with a strong and responsive research and development organization it can exploit expeditiously and intelligently breakthroughs made by others.

Defensive external flexibility is easier to achieve and easier to measure, whereas aggressive external flexibility offers the real

* By 'independent' we mean customers whose ability and desire to buy are determined by economic trends which do not usually move together, such as consumer expenditures for durable goods and the defence budget.

rewards. Most firms need to achieve a measure of the former, but only a few will have the type of management, the type of skills, and the resources to achieve the latter. It should be noted that concern with either form of external flexibility is a relatively new phenomenon – a product of the post-World War II period.

By contrast, concern with *internal* flexibility is as old as business

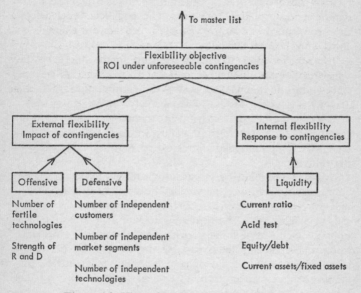

Figure 4.2. Hierarchy of the flexibility objective.

itself. Instead of seeking to minimize the size of the catastrophe (the fraction of the firm's sales affected), it seeks to provide a cushion for response to catastrophe. Although it confronts both large and small firms, the latter usually need and do exhibit the greater concern about internal flexibility and must have proportionally better internal ability to respond to catastrophes.

The traditional yardstick of internal flexibility is *liquidity* of the firm's resources, and among the measures are the current ratio, the acid test (an extreme measure of flexibility which measures 'instant response'), the debt to equity ratio, and the fixed to current asset ratio. For high flexibility the debt to equity ratio should be low to provide the firm with reserve borrowing power. On the other hand, a large debt/equity ratio is a measure of the management's use of leverage to increase the efficiency of the firm and hence maximize the return to stockholders. This is another instance of the conflict between objectives, which must be resolved by the management.*

The hierarchy of the flexibility objective is shown on Figure 4.2. In the top box the catastrophes and the breakthroughs are lumped under the title of *unforeseeable contingencies*. The specific yardsticks are phrased so as to permit a largely quantitative measure. However, sound qualitative assessment of external flexibility is probably more important and reliable than efforts to assign numbers.

NON-ECONOMIC OBJECTIVES, RESPONSIBILITIES, AND CONSTRAINTS

The flexibility objective completes the hierarchy needed for practical elaboration of the central economic objective. While this objective is central and determining in the behaviour of a majority of firms, other influences are present in many firms, which modify the economic objective and sometimes even replace it as the focus. Because of their origin, these will be called non-economic influences, even though some of them directly influence the firm's search of profit. It is convenient to separate these into those generated by factors internal to the firm and those due to the external environment. We shall further classify (as defined in Chapter 3) these influences into operating objectives, responsibilities, and constraints. Since the responsibilities do not interact with the firm's choice of products and markets in the strategy formulation process, they can be treated as constraints. The

* A study of debt/equity ratios of large 'old line' firms in mature industries suggests at first glance that flexibility is frequently assigned a higher priority than the efficiency objective. However, this may be due more to a lack of entrepreneurial spirit within such firms than to a conscious assignment of priorities. This conclusion is supported by the fact that many such firms are veritable 'banks' with large cash and securities accounts.

distinction between constraints and objectives resides in the fact that the former represent the *limits* within which the firm must operate, whereas the latter are the *goals* which the firm strives to attain.[58]

Constraints and responsibilities severely limit the freedom of strategic action. Thus, for example, the recent trend in the American government's interpretation of the Sherman and Clayton Antitrust Acts has sharply limited the freedom of diversification for many firms. Similarly, a sizable philanthropic responsibility assumed by a firm, say, for support of a non-profit foundation can curtail the resources available for growth and expansion.*

One of the major sources of internal influence on the firm is the objectives and ambitions of its diverse participants. These are determined by a great many attributes of the participants' backgrounds such as cultural and religious upbringing, racial origin, economic status, age, and career ambitions. Another source may be certain institutional characteristics which have developed historically within the firm. For example, some firms have developed an unwritten but nevertheless carefully followed policy that none of its 'key' management people ever get fired. Once the person gains admission into the 'key' club, he is guaranteed job security till retirement.

As discussed earlier, Cyert and March argue that 'organizations do not have objectives, only people have objectives'.[64] They assert that while the firm may appear to have certain institutional characteristics, these can be traced back in time to the objectives and ambitions of earlier participating individuals who through a 'bargaining' process arrived at certain points of agreement. Later, these characteristics become institutionalized, because new management has either found them desirable for their own purposes or did not feel strongly enough to upset them.

Since our interest is not historical, but lies rather in the im-

* This second example is chosen intentionally to stretch the point. Actual record would indicate that most firms engage in philanthropy only when their earnings exceed substantially their expansion needs. This does indicate that economic objectives of the firm are given priority over non-economic influences.

mediate problem of providing assistance to decision makers, we shall recognize both institutional influences and personal objectives as affecting strategic decisions in the firm.

Institutional influences act largely as constraints on both objectives and strategy. The following institutional attitudes may have an important bearing on the objectives of the firm: job security for key personnel, racial bias in hiring and also in interfirm dealings, maintenance of a favourable image within the community, and promotion of personnel from within the firm.

One instance of the evolution of an institutional constraint to a point where it attains the status of the major operating objective has been described by Keynes:

> One of the most interesting and unnoticed developments of recent decades has been the tendency of big enterprise to socialize itself. A point arrives in the growth of a big institution – particularly a big railway or public utility enterprise, but also a big bank or big insurance company – at which the owners of the capital, i.e. the stockholders, are almost entirely dissociated from the management, with the result that the direct personal interest of the latter in the making of great profit becomes quite secondary. When this stage is reached, the general stability and reputation of the institution are more considered by the management than the maximum profit for the stockholders.[65]

OBJECTIVES OF INDIVIDUALS

Objectives of individuals stem from many diverse origins and are difficult to organize into a hierarchical relationship, such as was presented for the economic objectives. The processes by which individual drives combine into influences on the firm are not well understood. Cyert and March have described the general characteristics of what they call the 'bargaining process'. However, the actual mechanics of the process have not yet been fully explained.[66] For this reason we are forced to limit ourselves to a discussion of some of the most important personal influences on the firm.

1. *Maximum Current Earnings*. This personal objective can have a shattering effect on a firm when control is taken over by a person or a group with the explicit aim of siphoning out of the

firm most of its liquid or semiliquid assets. While generally regarded as unethical, the practice is prevalent, as exemplified by the takeover of the Capitol Transit Company by the Wolfson interests. For the duration of such ownership the sole objective is to maximize cash liquidity.

2. *Capital Gains.* During the high-growth phase of the electronics industry many new firms were started by owner-managers with the central objective of quick capital gains and the creation of a public image as a fast-growing, aggressive, competent firm. Since the owner's time horizon was short (up to the point of merger with a larger firm), strategic decision process was focused on short-term profitability to the exclusion of both the long-range and the flexibility objectives. Frequently, unwary purchasers of such companies found themselves in possession of an attractive but hollow shell of an electronics company.

Not all cases of pursuit of capital gains by influential owners lead to such drastic results. However, the near-term capital gains objective can and does place a primary priority on the proximate objective of the firm and on those parts of the long-term objective which contribute to an external image of a growth company.

Among the competing philosophies of objectives, some economists[67] argue that maximization of the market value of equity is the appropriate central objective for the firm. If one assumes that this is sought in the long run and that in the long term 'the truth will out' – the market will assess the firm for its long-term profitability prospects – then optimization of market value is equivalent to optimization of return on investment. The preceding remarks suggest, however, that in the short run very different objectives and strategies follow from the respective philosophies.

3. *Liquidity of Estate.* The desire to enhance the liquidity of the firm's equity frequently arises when controlling owners of closely held companies approach retirement age (or when the owner needs liquidity for other reasons). Two major alternatives to this end are to 'go public', or to merge the firm with another large one which is publicly held and widely traded. The former alternative requires that the firm be made attractive to the investing public which generally has a rather fragmentary and diffuse view of the

firm; the latter means attracting an individual buyer who will take a much closer and penetrating view of the property.

The respective alternatives will have generally similar, but specifically different, effects in the firm's objectives. If public issue is the object, emphasis will be placed on current profitability and on a 'growth image' created through the medium of public statements and reports. The aim is to make the firm attractive to individual and institutional investors. If a merger is being sought, more than just an 'image' is needed, because, before acquisition, the firm's operations will be subjected to a careful scrutiny of another management. The image must be backed by evidence of internal efficiency.

4. *Social Responsibility – Enlightened Self-interest.* A sense of personal obligation by management or owner to serve larger purposes of society is sometimes expressed in the form of *enlightened self-interest*. This is exemplified by the Weyerhaeuser Company, which undertook a national campaign to preserve national resources; the Caterpillar Tractor Company, which promotes better schools and roads for the nation; or Standard Oil of New Jersey, which campaigns to improve international relations. The consequences are not only improvements in social welfare, but also economic benefit for the firm. Since the respective policies stimulate growth and stability, the firm thus contributes to its own long-term growth objectives.

5. *Social Responsibility – Philanthropy.* Philanthropic objectives of influential participants lead to support of non-profit institutions, such as educational, medical, scientific foundations; public charities; and religious institutions. Since by definition, such activities have no direct relationship to the economic pursuit of the firm, they affect the firm's behaviour primarily through the siphoning effect they have on retained earnings and hence on availability of resources for growth and expansion. Unlike enlightened self-interest, whose size can be readily controlled, certain philanthropic obligations tend to become institutionalized. If such an obligation becomes a major source of income to a permanent institution, the price to the firm for cancelling the obligation may become very high in terms of adverse public reaction.

6. *Attitude toward Risk*. In firms in which management controls the strategic decision process (a situation found, for example, in large widely held companies with strong management representation on the board of directors), personalities, experience, training, and personal objectives of top managers will add up to different overall institutional attitudes toward risk. This may range from highly entrepreneurial risk-taking, such as may be evidenced by a young aggressive management which is 'on the make', to overtly conservative attitudes by older management which seeks to perpetuate itself until retirement age.[68]

Attitude toward risk is a major constraint which must be taken into account in formulating objectives and particularly in establishing their priorities. Many young staff management

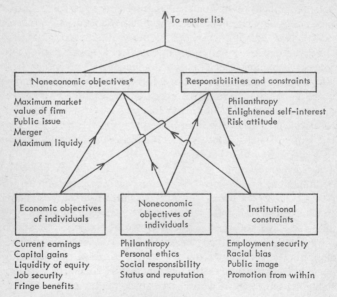

Figure 4.3. Hierarchy of internally generated non-economic influences.
(* Note that the term 'non-economic' means here 'not directly derivable from the firm's basic economic objective'. The impact of such an objective on firm's profit-seeking behaviour can be very far-reaching indeed.)

scientists complain that their superiors are unsympathetic to the recommendations submitted to them and 'do not understand the problem'. In actual fact, this attitude may reflect a particular risk-taking philosophy to which the decision maker feels entitled in view of the ultimate responsibility which he bears.

The rather complex preceding discussion of non-economic influences has been summarized for quick reference in Figure 4.3. For convenience, the personal objectives have been grouped into two categories: *personal economic objectives*, which includes maximization of current earnings, capital gains, liquidity and equity, fringe benefits, and job security; and *personal non-economic* objectives, which includes philanthropy, personal ethics, social responsibilities, social status, and reputation.

The listings are intended to be suggestive rather than exhaustive, since understanding of both the variables and the mechanism which determines the firm's non-economic objectives, responsibilities, and constraints is still imperfect and in need of much research. It is our hope that a real-world 'objectives setter' can find guidelines and suggestions in the map of Figure 4.3. The procedure is to single out non-economic influences within the firm which have a strong bearing on the economic objective, and then to assess the extent to which these affect the attributes and the priorities on the firm's master list of objectives.

THE PROCESS OF SETTING OBJECTIVES

An effort to establish realistic objectives for a business firm has led us to a complex structure of proxy objectives and sub-objectives. This complexity results from the practical limitations on evaluating long-term profitability of the firm and from the presence of non-economic objectives.

An overall hierarchy of the diverse objectives discussed in the preceding sections is summarized in Figure 4.4. We have tried to identify the principal yardsticks by which the objectives can be measured and also the mechanism by which non-economic objectives and constraints generated within the firm affect the economic objective. In extreme cases this effect was seen to be far-reaching to the point of displacing long-term profitability from

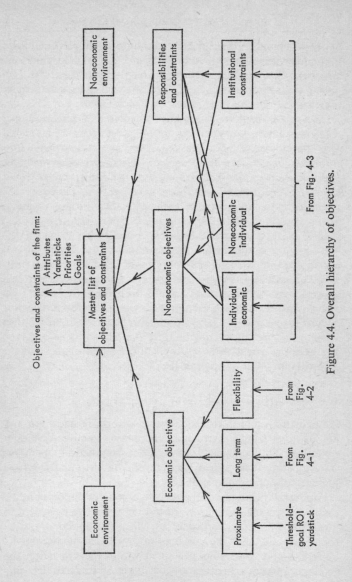

Figure 4.4. Overall hierarchy of objectives.

its central role in the firm and/or suppressing its relative priority. In a more normal case, the non-economic influences serve to enlarge the master list. As a minimum, they may have some effect on priorities and goal values. Failure to take account of such restrictions may incur unnecessary costs to the firm. As an example, some defence-orientated companies made repeated unsuccessful and costly efforts to enter areas of non-defence business in which they were basically non-competitive because of their very high wage scales. If the wage scales were recognized as a contractual constraint under which defence firms have to operate, the costs of unsuccessful tries would have been avoided.*

The preceding discussion outlined the steps in constructing a master list of constraints and objectives. The next steps are the assigning of relative priorities and goal values to each.

We have already discussed how some of the priorities are imposed by non-economic considerations. Three major economic variables affect priorities: 1. the firm's current and past performance, 2. the total resources available to the firm, and 3. the characteristics and opportunities in the external competitive environment.

If the firm happens to have pursued one of the objectives to the detriment of others, then there is presumptive evidence that reallocation of priorities is in order. For example, a profitable firm which has good growth prospects, but is a captive of a single customer, very likely needs emphasis on flexibility. A currently profitable firm faced with declining markets needs to put a major emphasis on long-term growth. A widely diversified and flexible firm which is not making any money [as was the case in General Motors at the close of Durant's era[69]] needs to curtail its diversification activities in favour of consolidation and near-term profitability.

One reason why these conclusions need to be regarded as tentative is the fact that availability of resources also affects priorities. A small firm trying to gain a toehold may have neither the financial nor the management resources to do more than

---

* It is useful to separate the effect of constraints discussed in this chapter from so-called 'strengths and weaknesses' which will be dealt with later.

concentrate on short-term profitability. When its current position is made secure, it can look ahead to joint emphasis on proximate and long-term objectives. At the mature stage it can give a high priority to flexibility. As discussed earlier, firms 'safe as houses', occupying near-monopolistic positions, can afford to put major focus on survival, or on 'general stability and reputation'.

However, size is not the only determinant of priorities. A very large firm may find its resources too limited to enjoy the luxury of high priority on all of the sub-objectives. One excellent example of this case is the Underwood Corporation, which attempted a broad-front recovery on all of the principal profitability character- istics; it attempted to regain current profitability, while moderniz- ing the product line for future growth, and at the same time diversifying into data processing. The failure of the company to pull out of the trouble prior to its acquisition by Olivetti appears to have been caused partly by this dilution of management and other resources.*

Finally, and very importantly, the characteristics of the product-market environment have a major effect on priorities. The concept of the industry life-cycle offers a convenient vehicle for discussion. In the early exploratory stages of an industry, the prevalent concern of the participants is external competitive strength and the use of newly available technology to establish new product lines and markets. As the industry becomes struc- tured, internal efficiency becomes the guiding objective, and the emphasis is on developing an effective and efficient business organization. Later, strongly competitive interactions may de- velop – particularly if the industry is taken over by a small num- ber of competent firms. At this point objectives are again focused on maintenance and enhancement of a strong position vis-à-vis competitors. As the industry approaches maturity, near-term potential becomes dimmed partly through saturation of demand and partly because of the very high costs of further market

* Apropos of this point it should be pointed out that some writers assert that firms do not pursue more than one major objective at a time, shifting attention in time from one objective to another. See, for example, Cyert and March.[70] To us this appears to be a convenient but an oversimplified assumption.

penetration at the expense of competitors. At this point major emphasis is placed on long-term growth and flexibility.

The preceding remarks clearly show that the choice of objectives is not free. The firm is free to select the basic philosophy, and it has freedom in assigning priorities to non-economic objectives. But when it comes to the economic priorities, the choice is dictated by a number of factors which are all beyond management control. The same is true of the selection of goals, as was already demonstrated in earlier sections.

Thus realistic objectives cannot be arbitrarily decreed in a smoke-filled boardroom. They must be developed through a continuing interaction of objectives and other elements of the strategic problem. A detailed schematic of this interaction must await later chapters after the other key elements of strategy have been defined and introduced. However, to give substance to the process, a partial schematic is shown in Figure 4.5. It starts with a

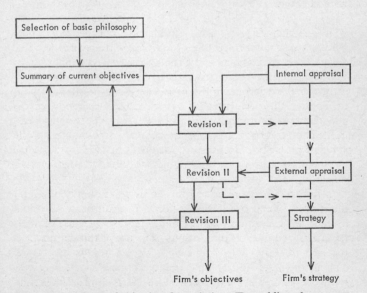

Figure 4.5. Process of objectives formulation. (Dotted lines denote part of process which has been oversimplified for this schematic.)

choice of the basic philosophy. Next, the firm's current objectives are summarized. If these do not exist in explicit form, they should be inferred to the extent possible from the firm's past behaviour and supplemented with 'smoke-filled room' tentative decisions. In parallel with this effort an *appraisal* of the firm's position is instituted in a manner to be discussed later. Next, the current objectives are evaluated in the light of the appraisal and adjusted accordingly. For example, the current activity may be addressed to an almost exclusive pursuit of current profitability, but the appraisal may show that long-term prospects are poor because of the firm's failure to develop a growth base. At that point the long-term objective would be given a large increase in emphasis.

If a decision is made as a part of the appraisal that the firm should diversify, or if the management risk attitude is such that it wishes to explore outside opportunities regardless of present prospects, then *external appraisal* of available opportunities will be made. Again, the objectives will be reviewed both from priorities and goals. Upon selection of a particular diversification strategy, a final review, this time primarily of the goals, will take place. At that point operating objectives are ready for use.

Objectives are a management tool with many potential uses. In the operating problem they can be used for establishing performance standards and objectives for all organizational levels, for appraisal of performance, and for control decisions. In the administrative problem they can be used to diagnose deficiencies in the organizational structure. In our main area of interest, the strategic problem, objectives are used as yardsticks for decisions on changes, deletions, and additions to the firm's product-market posture.

In this role the mere evaluation of an opportunity on several dimensions of the objectives vector is not sufficient. The final acceptance or rejection requires an *overall* relative figure of merit to be assigned to each opportunity. The use of threshold values for each objective helps somewhat, since it results in a quick elimination of obviously unacceptable opportunities. The presence of priorities helps too, since they emphasize certain characteristics required of an opportunity, such as high growth rate, or a contribution to flexibility. However, at the 'moment of truth' the final yes or no includes a balanced evaluation of all the relevant factors.

This problem of selecting opportunities which are measured by a number of incommensurate components of an objectives vector does not have a satisfactory solution at present.* Among a variety of approaches which have been proposed by management scientists, each has unresolved problems which precludes its unquestioning acceptance by the decision maker. However, if he is willing to question them and to accept the results for the insights they provide, the manager can obtain substantial assistance from such techniques. In this effort he will require help from a competent management scientist, who not only will perform the evaluation, but also will point to the limitations in the underlying assumptions. A specific method for evaluating incommensurate components of objectives will be developed in Chapter 9.

* We assumed the burden of this problem in Chapter 3 when we decided to face the real-world fact that data are not available to produce a single index number to represent the firm's objective.

CHAPTER 5

Synergy and Capability Profiles

'Speak English!' said the Eaglet. 'I don't know the meaning of half those long words, and what's more, I don't believe you do either!'

LEWIS CARROLL

THE PROBLEM

IN this chapter we begin to explore *synergy*, which is one of the major components of the firm's product-market strategy. It is concerned with the desired characteristics of fit between the firm and its new product-market entries. In business literature it is frequently described as the '2 + 2 = 5' effect to denote the fact that the firm seeks a product-market posture with a combined performance that is greater than the sum of its parts.

In item three on the list of requirements presented in Chapter 2 for a strategic decision method, we described synergy as a measure of joint effects. It will be recalled that this requirement arises from practical rather than theoretical needs. If it were practically possible in each instant to compute the *marginal* cash flows into and out of the firm for each new project, the requirement would not exist, since this aspect of project evaluation would be adequately covered by capital investment theory. Nor would it exist if it were possible to compute quickly and efficiently the new flows for the entire firm each time a new project came along.*

As a substitute for these infeasible approaches, we shall derive a method for qualitative estimation of joint effects. In the process it will be shown that measurement of synergy is similar in many

---

* It would appear, at first glance, that this could be done by 'computerizing' the internal operations of the firm, i.e. by programming its planning process on a high-speed computer. While this step certainly provides for some of the synergistic interactions, it still falls short of the total requirement. To meet the complete requirement we shall require much better models of the firm than are currently available. In particular, models are needed which can measure the potential of the firm as a result of radical changes in its product-market posture.

ways to what is frequently called 'evaluation of strengths and weaknesses'. In synergy, *joint* effects are measured between two product-markets; in strength and weakness evaluation, the firm's competences are rated relative to some desired performance level. The former contributes to the decision to make a new entry; the latter, to the decision to exploit certain strengths or to remedy certain deficiencies within the firm. Thus the difference is largely one of viewpoint.

With this in mind we shall develop an estimation technique which is applicable for both purposes. This will be accomplished by means of *capability profiles*. At the end of the chapter we shall have a multipurpose technique which can be used to 1. evaluate any internal strengths and weaknesses within the firm, 2. derive synergy characteristics which the firm can use in its search for opportunities, and 3. measure the synergy potential between the firm and a possible acquisition.

CONCEPT OF SYNERGY

Use of simple mathematical symbols is helpful for a quick summary of the meaning of synergy. Each product-market makes a contribution to the overall profitability of the firm. Each product brings in annual sales of S dollars. Operating costs of O dollars are incurred for labour, materials, overhead, administration, and depreciation. To develop the product, to provide facilities and equipment, and to set up a distribution network, an investment of I dollars must be made in product development, tooling, buildings, machinery, inventories, etc.

The annual rate of return, ROI, on product P_1 can be written in the form

$$\text{ROI} = \frac{S_1 - O_1}{I_1}$$

Expressed in words, the formula states that the return on investment from a product can be obtained by dividing the difference between operating revenues and costs during a period by the average investment which is needed to support the product. A similar expression can be written for all products in the product line: $P_1, P_2, \ldots, P_n$.

73

If all the products are unrelated in any way, the total sales of the firm will be

$$S_T = S_1 + S_2 + \ldots + S_n$$

And similarly for operating costs and investment

$$O_T = O_1 + \ldots + O_n$$
$$I_T = I_1 + I_2 + \ldots + I_n$$

The return on the investment for the firm as a whole will be

$$(\text{ROI})_T = \frac{S_T - O_T}{I_T}$$

This condition obtains whenever the revenues, the operating costs, and the investments are unrelated. Therefore, their totals can be obtained through simple additions. In practice this is very nearly true in an investment firm which holds unrelated securities, or in a holding company in which there is no interaction among the operating units. A picture of the total profitability is obtained through a simple consolidation of the individual statements.

In a majority of firms, advantages of scale exist under which a large firm with the same total sales as a number of small firms can operate at a cost which is lower than the sum of the operating costs for the separate enterprises. The investment in a large firm can be similarly lower than a simple sum of the respective investments. Using symbols, this is equivalent to saying that for

$$S_s = S_T$$

we have

$$O_s \leqslant O_T$$
$$I_s \leqslant I_T$$

where subscript s denotes the respective quantities for an integrated firm and subscript T, the sum for independent enterprises.* As a result, the potential return on investment for an integrated firm is higher than the composite return which would be obtained if the same dollar volumes for its respective products were produced by a number of independent firms:

$$(\text{ROI})_s > (\text{ROI})_T$$

* The symbol $\leqslant$ means less than or equal to; the symbol $\geqslant$ means greater than or equal to.

A similar argument can, of course, be made by keeping the total investment fixed. In this case

$$S_s \geqslant S_T$$
$$O_s \leqq O_T$$
$$I_s = I_T$$

For a given level of investment, a firm with a complete product line can usually realize the advantages of higher total revenues and/or lower operating costs than competing independent firms.

The consequences of this joint effect are clearly very far-reaching. A firm which takes care to select its products and markets so as to optimize the effect has great flexibility in choosing its competitive stance. It can gain a larger share of the market by lowering prices, it can choose to make a larger investment in research and development than its competitors, or it can maximize its ROI and attract growth capital to the firm. All this can be done while remaining fully competitive with firms whose product-markets are not as carefully chosen.

TYPES OF SYNERGY

This effect which can produce a combined return on the firm's resources greater than the sum of its parts is frequently referred to as '2 + 2 = 5'. We shall call this effect *synergy*.[71] One way to classify the several types of synergy is in terms of the components of the ROI formula:

1. *Sales Synergy*. This can occur when products use common distribution channels, common sales administration, or common warehousing. Opportunity for tie-in sales offered by a complete line of related products increases the productivity of the sales force. Common advertising, sales promotion, past reputation can all have multiple returns for the same dollar spent.

2. *Operating Synergy*. This is the result of higher utilization of facilities and personnel, spreading of overhead, advantages of common learning curves, and large-lot purchasing.

3. *Investment Synergy*. This can result from joint use of plant, common raw materials inventories, transfer of research and

development from one product to another, common tooling, common machinery.

4. *Management Synergy*. Although not immediately apparent from the formula, this type is an important contributor to the total effect. As will be shown below, management in different types of industry faces different strategic, organizational, and operating problems. If upon entering a new industry management finds the new problems to be similar to the ones it has encountered in the past, it is in a position to provide forceful and effective guidance to the newly acquired venture. Since competent top-level management is a scarce commodity, very positive enhancement of performance can result in the combined enterprise. Thus synergy will be strong.

If, on the other hand, the problems in the acquired area are new and unfamiliar, not only will positive synergy be low, but there is a distinct danger of a negative effect of top-management decisions. For example, management of a firm in the defence industry would be at an actual disadvantage if it attempts, without prior experience, to assume responsibility for pricing and advertising decisions in a highly competitive consumer area, such as the cigarette or the automobile industry.

This example points to the fact that management synergy, as well as the other types, can be negative as well as positive. An attempt at joint use of a facility which is not suited for manufacturing of a new product (e.g. use of aircraft factories for consumer aluminium products), or of an organization which is not set up to perform a new function (e.g. use of a consumer sales organization to sell to industrial customers) can result in total profitability which is *lower* than the combined profitability of two independent operations.

Table 5.1 demonstrates the possibility of negative synergy through a comparison of competences in the principal functional areas found in typical firms in different industry groups. For purposes of comparison we are assuming that a firm in one of the groups shown in the first column diversifies into an industry group shown in the first line.

It is seen that the best transfer of functional competence will occur in general management, where many practices and skills in

TABLE 5.1* *Functional Synergy between Industry Groups*

| Diversifying industry | Functional capability | New industry | | |
		Defense-space	Producers	Consumers
Defense-space	GM	High	High	Moderate
	R&D	High	Moderate	Low
	Mfg.	High	Low	Negative
	Mkt.	High	Low	Negative
Producers	GM	High	High	Moderate
	R&D	Moderate	High	Low
	Mfg.	Low	High	Low
	Mkt.	Low	High	Low
Consumers	GM	Moderate	Moderate	High
	R&D	Low	Low	High
	Mfg.	Negative	Low	High
	Mkt.	Negative	Low	High

Legend
  GM – general management
  R&D – research and development
  Mfg. – manufacturing
  Mkt. – marketing

accounting, finance, industrial relations, and public relations are common among industries. However, even here the differences in the competitive environment and in basic resource allocation problems have led us to give unequal ratings to different pairs of industrial areas. In manufacturing and marketing where organizational forms, cost controls, and individual skills become more specialized, greater differences in synergy appear among the groups. The differences become so great between space defence and consumer groups as to create potentially negative synergy.

It should be noted that the above table describes *potential* (rather than actual) synergy. Whether the indicated joint effects will, in fact, materialize depends on the manner in which the new acquisition is integrated into the parent organization. This problem of management control will be discussed in Chapter 8.

* This table is from H. I. Ansoff and J. F. Weston, 'Merger Objectives and Organization Structure', *Review of Economics and Business*, August 1963, pp. 49–58.

START-UP SYNERGY AND OPERATING SYNERGY

As discussed above, the synergistic effect can be measured in either of two ways: by estimating the cost economics to the firm from a joint operation for a given level or revenue, or by estimating the increase in net revenue for a given level of investment. In this section we shall take the first approach and discuss the nature of synergy through analysis of cost economies and diseconomies.

Acquisition of a new product-market area goes through two successive phases, start-up and operating. In addition to identifiable physical costs, such as the costs of facilities and inventories, the costs associated with start-up include the highly intangible costs of learning a new kind of business: setting up a new organization, establishing new rules and procedures, hiring new skills and competences, paying for mistakes in developing organizational relationships and for early bad decisions made in unfamiliar business environment, and costs of gaining customer acceptance. Although these are one-time costs, most of them are not capitalized, but charged to operating expense during the start-up period. They are difficult to pinpoint, since many of them are not identified (no firm is likely to have a special account labelled 'management blunders made in start-up'), but are evident only indirectly through substandard operating efficiencies.* During the period in which they are incurred they put the firm at a disadvantage with respect to the established competitors in the field, since the latter no longer incur any of these costs.

Whether the firm will, in fact, have to incur these start-up costs depends on how well its skills and resources are matched to the requirements of the new product-market area. If the required new capabilities are very different from those of the firm, then, as discussed earlier, cost dis-economies may result in any of the major functional areas. Thus start-up in new business can have potentially negative as well as positive synergy; a firm with positive synergy will have a competitive advantage over a firm which lacks it.

* This is one major reason for the difficulty encountered in determining marginal cash flows for new product-market entries.

In addition to the direct and hidden dollar costs, start-up in a new product-market often carries a penalty for time delay. A firm which has the requisite skills and resources, such as suitable production facilities or the appropriate distribution channels for a new market, can quickly transfer them to new activities and thus get a head start on firms which have to build from scratch. The timing advantage in synergy becomes particularly desirable when the new entry is in a dynamic fast-growth stage. Rapid response will have less significance if the firm is considering an entry into a latent demand market (such as RCA's early entry into colour television), or if the new market is stable and slow growing (which would be the case if, for some strange reason, a new firm sought an entry into the textile industry).

Thus, during the start-up phase, synergy can occur in two forms: in the form of dollar savings to the firm thanks to the existence of competences appropriate to the new line of business, and in the form of time savings in becoming fully competitive.

The second category of costs incurred in a new entry is the costs of a going concern: the operating costs and the investment required to support the operation. Here two basic effects operate to produce synergy. One is the advantage of scale – many operations will produce at a lower unit cost when the total volume is increased. For example, purchasing in large quantities offers the advantage of discounts; production in large quantities makes possible more efficient methods and procedures and hence lower direct costs. Many other well-known examples can be given.

A more subtle effect in synergy is a distribution of the burden of overhead expenses over a number of products. This arises from the fact that most overhead functions require a certain minimum level of effort for a wide range of business volume. If volume can be added through a type of diversification which makes use of the existing overhead services, economies will be effected in both the new and the old business. For example, a sales management and administration function must be staffed regardless of whether the firm has one product or a full line; the same research must be conducted regardless of whether it supports one or many products (so long as the products are all based on the same technology).

If top -management talent in a firm is not fully utilized in

79

running the present business, and if its training and experience are relevant, it can provide the most critical ingredient to the new operation. Unfortunately, this potentially strongest component of synergy is also most difficult to measure. Many diversification histories can be cited in which an erroneous estimate was made, either through failure to realize that top management was already fully committed and that new responsibilities resulted in a thin spread of talent or through failure to realize that new business called for different types of talent and experience and that synergy, in fact, did not exist.

In general, synergy effects during start-up will go hand in hand with operating synergy. However, the strength of the respective effects will differ. For example, a firm with a fully developed position in an area of consumer merchandising, say, in clothing, would have a strong bid for an entry into the toy industry, where similar merchandising experience and talent are required. However, the new entry would require setting up and operating different sales organizations, different manufacturing facilities, different purchases, and different product development. Thus while start-up synergy will be strong in the advantages of timing and basic business know-how, operating synergy will be limited to sales administration and to general management. On the other hand, a firm in women's clothing which adds a line of swimming apparel would have both strong start-up and operating synergy.

SYMMETRY AND JOINT EFFECTS

For convenience the preceding discussion has been presented from the viewpoint of the advantages which the diversifying firm can offer to a new product-market entry. It should be made clear that the effects of synergy are symmetric. While the diversifying firm offers benefits to the new product line, it may receive substantial benefits in return. For example, while the parent may strengthen the new subsidiary's research capability, the latter may offer new marketing outlets for the parent's products.

Further, while the viewpoint of cost and investment economics used above is convenient, it fails to account for a full range of potential synergistic benefits. Rather than permit lower cost in support of previous sales volumes, synergy is most frequently sought as a quick way to accelerate growth without additional major investments. This may come from the mutual contributions of *existing* skills and capacities which otherwise might take long to acquire and for which start-up premiums might have to be paid.

A less frequent, but much sought after, effect occurs when by combining resources the joint firm gains access to product-markets to which neither could previously gain access without a major investment. Thus the merger of the Remington Rand Company, an office machine company, with Sperry, an electronics concern, provided a foundation for the electronic computer entry by Sperry-Rand. The merger of Puget Sound Bridge and Dry-dock, a shipbuilding company, into Lockheed, which is highly sophisticated in many fields of technology, provided a basis for the former's efforts to get into atomic submarine business.

A FRAMEWORK FOR EVALUATION OF SYNERGY

In principle, all synergistic effects can be mapped on one of three variables: increased volume of dollar revenue to the firm from sales, decreased operating costs, and decreased investment requirements. All three are viewed in the perspective of time; therefore, a fourth synergistic effect is acceleration of the respective changes in the three variables. If this mapping could be carried out in practice, the total effect of synergy could be reflected in the return on investment formula (or some other cash-flow scheme).

In practice, the mapping is frequently not possible, particularly when strategic moves contemplate product-markets in which the firm has little previous experience. Under such conditions, although the primary variables affecting synergy can be identified, as we have done above, it is not possible to quantify and combine their effects.*

As was discussed in Chapter 2, this problem is not unique to measurement of synergy. It occurs in many other parts of the strategic decision process. Our general approach to it in this book

---

* Part of the reason is the simple fact that models relating these variables quantitatively are largely unavailable.

TABLE 5.2 Measurement of Synergy of a New Product-market Entry

Functional area / Effects due to pooling of competences — Symmetry effects	Startup economies			Operating economies		Expansion of present sales	New product and market areas	Overall synergy
	Investment	Operating	Timing	Investment	Operating			
General management and finance Contribution to parent Contribution to new entry Joint opportunities								
Research and development Contribution to parent Contribution to new entry Joint opportunities								
Marketing Contribution to parent Contribution to new entry Joint opportunities								
Operations Contribution to parent Contribution to new entry Joint opportunities								

is to construct a separate measurement of each important effect and, in a later chapter, to construct a method for applying these measures jointly to overall evaluation of a project.

A framework for assessing synergy is shown in Table 5.2, which in effect summarizes the developments of this chapter. Synergy effects are first grouped by the primary functional areas of the firm: general management, research and development, marketing, and operations (which includes manufacturing, purchasing, inventory control, distribution, and warehousing). Some firms may prefer a finer breakdown of categories. For example, firms which deal heavily in money, securities, and financing will benefit by separating finance from general management. Within each functional area three possible symmetric effects are considered:
1. The contribution which the new product-market entry can make to the firm. (This is a very important effect when the entry is sought through an acquisition of a firm which is comparable in size to the parent. The effect may be negligible when the acquisition is small or the entry is through internal product development.) 2. The contribution from the parent to the entry. 3. Further product-market moves which the two will be able to undertake as a result of the consolidation.[72]

The columns in the table list the variables to be considered in connexion with each of the categories. The headings of the columns list the various ways in which synergistic effects may manifest themselves and are self-explanatory in the light of the preceding discussion. It will be noted that a column labelled 'investment' is provided under both start-up and operating synergy. The intent is that a firm will use the former to assess one-time learning costs which do not result in tangible physical facilities, such as marketing start-up costs. The investment entries under operations reflect economics of acquisition of tangible physical assets.

The entries in Table 5.2 should be measurements of the strength of a particular effect. Wherever possible, they should be assigned a numerical value, such as 'reduction of 40,000 square feet in plant requirements' or '20 per cent increase of sales on same investment base'. Failing this, the entries will be relative qualitative ratings. A column is provided for the overall synergy rating, most likely a qualitative one, for each functional area. These in turn can be combined into one overall rating for the prospective entry. Before discussing these entries we need to consider a problem very similar to estimation of synergy, which is frequently called estimation of the firm's strengths and weaknesses.

STRENGTHS AND WEAKNESSES

Management literature dealing with problems of product-market change suggests that one of the early steps following the formulation of objectives should be an analysis of 'strengths and weaknesses' or, as more appropriately described by Staudt, 'an audit of the tangible and intangible resources for diversification'.[73]

The audit has two purposes. First, it can identify deficiencies in the firm's present skills and resources which can be corrected *short* of diversification. Second, it can identify strengths from which the firm can lead in pursuing diversification and/or deficiencies which it may wish to correct *through* diversification.

The strengths from which the firm wishes to lead are readily identified from the preceding discussion as the *synergy* component of the firm's strategy. By searching out opportunities which match its strengths, the firm can optimize the synergistic effects. Thus the problem of strengths and weaknesses and the problem of synergy are seen to be related.

It is also apparent that the estimates made in both problems are relative. In the first part of the audit the firm's deficiencies are compared with those of its successful competitors. In the second part the strengths can only be identified relative to the industries into which the firm seeks to diversify. Thus, for example, a superior competence in design of lightweight strong but expensive structures which is a 'strength' in the aircraft-missile industry, is a weakness when applied to design of industrial machinery (as was shown by the venture of Bell Aircraft into industrial wheelbarrows).

In order to accommodate synergy and strengths and weaknesses within the same analytic framework, we shall use the method of profile comparison. As the first step we shall develop the framework for a *capability profile* which rates a particular pattern of skills and facilities relative to some reference level. We do this by first constructing a grid which matches functional areas in the firm against its skills and competences, and then by providing a checklist for entries into the grid.

GRID OF COMPETENCES

The framework we seek must possess two key features. To be widely applicable, it must be constructed in terms of competence areas which are common to most industries; to be applicable to a single firm, these areas must list specific skills and resources which differentiate between success and failure in different types of business. In other words, we are seeking a common framework with differentiated contents within it. Since a fully integrated manufacturing firm has the most comprehensive framework of capabilities, we shall use it as a point of reference. Frameworks for analysis of firms in trade, finance, and services can be obtained through simplification of the general model.

The individual skills and resources can be organized along the same major functional areas as in the preceding table:

1. *Research and development* – which we define to encompass the entire process of creating a marketable product. Included are pure and applied research, construction of breadboards and prototypes, industrial design, and preparation of manufacturing drawings. Also included is development of manufacturing processes and techniques. Market research is included insofar as it is concerned with determining the price-performance characteristics of the product and the size and structure of the market.

2. *Operations* is concerned with procurement of raw materials, scheduling and controlling production, tooling, manufacturing engineering, quality control, inventory, and manufacturing the product.

3. *Marketing* is taken as a broad activity concerned with creating product acceptance, advertising, sales promotion, selling, distributing the product (including transportation and warehousing), contract administration, sales analysis, and, very importantly, servicing the product.

4. *General management and finance* is taken to include three areas of activity:

a. Determining the overall pattern of relationships between the firm and its environment. This includes determination of strategy and the total resource allocation, acquisition of new product-market positions for the firm, obtaining necessary financing, and maintaining public relations.

b. Providing integrated decision making, guidance, and control to the functional areas – particularly in areas of pricing, inventory levels, production levels, capital expenditures, and individual functional goals.

c. Providing various staff services to the functional areas, such as accounting, industrial relations, personnel training, and performing functions which are most efficiently carried out at centralized levels, such as purchasing.

Within each of these functional areas we recognize four categories of skills and resources:

1. *Facilities and equipment.*

2. *Personnel skills.*

3. *Organizational capabilities* – this includes specialized organizational units, such as mass production or large systems management, established standards, policies and procedures for performance of specialized functions.

4. *Management capabilities* – this is described by the types of decisions and actions for which the management is specially qualified by virtue of training, experience, and present responsibilities. For example, an ability to live with cyclical demand conditions, such as those encountered in the machine tool industry or the textile industry, is a management skill acquired with experience; another is knowledge and understanding of doing complex prime contractor work for the government.

CONTENTS OF THE GRID

The dual classification presented above offers a refined grid for assessing a firm's competences. We must next concern ourselves with the contents. The purpose is to develop a master list of entries which will contain the different kinds of capabilities encountered in American industry. In view of the great variety of competitive structures such a list cannot be made exhaustive. The purpose is, rather, to provide a master checklist which can be refined by each firm. The following discussion is organized around typical characteristics of three principal industrial groups in the United States economy: producers of durables and non-durables, consumers of durables and non-durables, and products and systems for military combat and for space missions. Each appears to have a different 'success function' – a different combination of capabilities required of successful competitors.

A major difficulty in determining the success function of consumer products is that customer acceptance is seldom based on measurable performance characteristics of the product. More frequently it is determined by a complex of factors (the interaction of which is imperfectly understood): apparent performance advantage conveyed to the customer through advertising and sales promotion, price advantage, ready availability of product, fashion, social pressure, artificial obsolescence of preceding products. Since customer acceptance is relatively insensitive to actual performance characteristics, and since quality differences among brands tend to be small, capabilities which are of greatest importance in consumer business lie in the area of merchandising skills – in advertising, product styling, promotion, distribution, and selling. Since demand is sensitive to price, cost-conscious engineering design philosophy is also an important factor.

In industrial products the interaction tends to be somewhat less complex. The critical factor in product acceptance is its economic justification: demonstrable ability of the product to make money for the buyer (in the form of savings or increased income). Price differential is important, but is related to quality. It is not uncommon in industry to pay a high price for a proven and reliable product. Of great importance is a demonstrated ability of the product to perform reliably. Among key competitive skills in industry are knowledge of customer's economic justification levels and an ability to design to them, ability to translate new technology into reliable products, special process and manufacturing competences, patent protection, sensitivity to customer needs and requirements, and an ability to provide quick and efficient product service.

End products sold to military and space missions succeed primarily if their performance capabilities are in excess of anything which had been previously available. In addition, they must be virtually failure-free during intermittent periods of all-out performance under extreme environmental conditions. A major competitive skill is an ability to apply the most advanced state of the art to products and systems. Organizational competence to manage development and manufacturing of technologically advanced, highly complex systems is another central skill. A very substantial share of military and space business differs from the industrial in that the customer usually buys a design (and a very preliminary one at that) instead of an existing product. This puts emphasis on a very special kind of marketing competence required in the U.S. Department of Defence (DOD) and National Aeronautics and Space Administration (NASA) business. Technical quality of the design, past performance on similar contracts, technical and scientific reputation, and geopolitical advantages enjoyed by the firm all play an important role in marketing. The salesman is frequently a middleman between engineering and the customer, rather than an active merchandiser.

While these three groups exhibit important differences, their boundaries are not sharply drawn and there are many overlaps. Many industrial products (components, for example) have competitive characteristics closely resembling those in the consumer business. The DOD and NASA customers buy vast quantities of industrial-type material. The large and growing non-military government market (Federal, state, municipal) has features in common with both military and industrial markets.

In filling out the grid, it is therefore desirable to forego reference to the respective groups and instead to compile a checklist of characteristics of the facilities, skills, organization, and management which may be encountered. The result of such an approach is shown in Table 5.3. An effort was made to make this list comprehensive enough to enable each firm to find items which describe the pattern of its major competences. It is to be expected, however, that many firms will identify additional entries which apply to their particular cases.

As an example, use of the checklist by an American firm in road-building machinery may single out the following distinctive entries. In the *facilities and equipment* column: high-bay assembly plant, medium-precision large general-purpose machine tools, up-to-date materials test laboratory, large heavy-duty test truck for completed machines, nation-wide direct sales and service offices. Under *personnel skills*: engineering skills in design and manufacture of rugged, medium-tolerance, large machinery, requiring marginal maintenance. *Organizational skills*: job shop for handling large medium-tolerance assembly, strong sales, and field service. *Management skills*: knowledge of dealing with Federal government, states, and municipalities, experience in running a cyclical business subject to the variations of capital goods cycle and vagaries of Federal and state budgets.

COMPETENCE AND COMPETITIVE PROFILES

The example describes a part of what we shall call the firm's *competence profile*. It is a list of the major skills and competences in the firm (identified with the aid of Table 5.3) rated with respect to other firms which have the same capabilities. Although most firms would prefer to make the comparison with their own competitors, it is desirable to rate the respective capabilities also with respect to other industries in which they exist. Thus the high-bay large product assembly facilities in the example above would also be found in firms which build railway equipment rolling stock and in materials-handling firms. In assigning the relative ratings some firms may prefer to use a simple two-valued strength or weakness classification. Others would rank the capabilities as outstanding, average, or weak; still others may construct bar-chart profiles.*

The competence profile is the basic reference profile for the firm. It is relatively permanent and will need updating only when major changes occur in the capabilities. The competence profile is

* Similar types of profiles have been used by some firms in evaluation of research and development proposals.

TABLE 5.3 *Checklist for Competitive and Competence Profiles*

	Facilities and equipment	Personnel skills	Organizational capabilities	Management capabilities
General management & finance	Data processing equipment	Depth of general management Finance Industrial Relations Legal Personnel recruitment and training Accounting Planning	Multi-divisional structure Consumer financing Industrial financing Planning and control Automated business data processing	Investment management Centralized control Large systems management Decentralized control R & D intensive business Capital-equipment intensive business Merchandising intensive business Cyclical business Many customers Few customers
Research and development	Special lab equipment General lab equipment Test facilities	Areas of specialization Advanced research Applied research Product design: industrial consumer military specifications Systems design Industrial design: consumer industrial	Systems development Product development industrial consumer process Military specifications compliance	Utilization of advanced state of the art Application of current state of the art Cost-performance optimization

Operations	General machine shop Precision machinery Process equipment Automated production Large high-bay facilities Controlled environment	Machine operation Tool making Assembly Precision machinery Close tolerance work Process operation Product planning	Mass production Continuous flow process Batch process Job shop Large complex product assembly Subsystems integration Complex product control Quality control Purchasing	Operation under cyclic demand Military specifications quality Tight cost control Tight scheduling
Marketing	Warehousing Retail outlets Sales offices Service offices Transportation equipment	Door-to-door selling Retail selling Wholesale selling Direct industry selling Department of Defense selling Cross-industry selling Applications engineering Advertising Sales promotion Servicing Contract administration Sales analysis	Direct sales Distributor chain Retail chain Consumer service organization Industrial service organization Department of Defense product support Inventory distribution and control	Industrial marketing Consumer merchandising Department of Defense marketing State and municipality marketing

a strength and weakness profile only relative to specific areas of competences and skills. It does not necessarily denote strengths and weaknesses with respect to a particular product-market position, since different industries require different balances of capabilities. The major use of the competence profile is in assessment of this balance in four different parts of the strategic problem.

1. *Internal Appraisal.* As will be discussed in detail in Chapter 8, one of the early stages in strategy formulation is to assess the firm's capability to meet the objectives without a change in strategy. For this purpose a *competitive profile* is conducted which presents the capability pattern of the most successful competitors in the industry.* The competence and the competitive profiles are now superimposed to determine the areas in which the firm is either outstanding or deficient. *These are the strengths and weaknesses relative to the present product-market posture.*

2. *External Appraisal.* In a later step in strategy formulation, a broad field of outside industries is surveyed to determine attractive areas for the firm. A part of the evaluation will measure the growth and profitability characteristics of the various industries; another part measures the synergy potential between the firm and each new industry, since synergy determines the firm's ability to make a successful and profitable entry. This requires a competitive profile for each industry, describing the pattern of skills required for success. Such profiles can be constructed through a combined use of general industry data and competence profiles of the most successful firms in the industry. Superposition of our firm's competence profile with the respective competitive profiles measures the 'fit' with each new industry and hence the chances of a successful entry.

3. *Synergy Component of Strategy.* In Chapter 9 product-market strategy of the firm will be determined through several key components, each of which specifies rules for search and for evaluation of opportunities. Synergy is one of these components. To derive it, a procedure like the above is used, but the compe-

---

* If the firm is already diversified, several competitive profiles may be needed, one for each distinct product-market line.

tence profile is now compared with competitive profiles for a few selected industries. The major relative strengths and weaknesses of the firm are identified and specified as rules for search. The management has a choice of an *aggressive strategy*, in which the strengths are used as search criteria, or a *defensive strategy*, in which the search is directed toward remedying the weaknesses, or both. The strategy will be chosen subject to availability of opportunities which can match the firm in areas of both strength and weakness.

4. *Evaluation of Individual Opportunities.* Once search has uncovered a promising acquisition or a new product, a final evaluation must be made. A part of this evaluation is a measurement of synergy as a contributing factor to potential joint profitability. This requires completion of Table 5.2 presented earlier in this chapter. Profiles of the firm and of the acquisition are constructed and superimposed. Then:

a. The resulting pattern is compared with the competitive profile of a successful competitor in the firm's own business developed in item 1. above to determine whether the pattern of reinforcements will make any significant contribution to the parent firm's competitive position. The results can be used to determine the entries in the line 'contribution to parent' in Table 5.2.

b. The superimposed profiles are similarly compared with a profile of a successful firm in the new entry's industry, thus giving material for the line in the table labelled 'contribution to new entry'.

c. Finally superimposed profiles are compared with typical profiles developed under 2. above to see whether the combination of the two firms' skills will provide an entry into an industry which neither could enter above. This provides data for the line in Table 5.2 labelled 'joint opportunities'.

This procedure of using paired profiles to fill in Table 5.2 is laborious and should be used primarily at the 'short strokes' of an acquisition. For a preliminary analysis, profiles can usually be dispensed with and Table 5.2 filled in on a judgement basis.

CHAPTER 6

Concept of Strategy

Strategy is when you are out of ammunition, but keep right on
firing so that the enemy won't know. *Author unknown*

THE PROBLEM

DURING the past ten years the idea of strategy has received increasing recognition in management literature. Numerous papers
have appeared dealing with product line strategy, marketing
strategy, diversification strategy, and business strategy.[74] This
interest grew out of a realization that a firm needs a well-defined
scope and growth direction, that objectives alone do not meet this
need, and that additional decision rules are required if the firm is
to have orderly and profitable growth. Such decision rules and
guidelines have been broadly defined as *strategy* or, sometimes,
as the *concept of the firm's business*.[75]

It will be recalled from discussion in Chapter 2 that capital
investment theory makes no use of the concept of strategy. The
need for it arises from characteristics which are peculiar to the
strategic problem: the fact that a firm needs direction and focus in
its search for and creation of new opportunities and the fact that
it is to the firm's advantage to seek entries with strong synergistic
potential.

The first two sections of this chapter are devoted to developing
a concept of strategy which 1. provides a broad concept of the
firm's business, 2. sets forth specific guidelines by which the firm
can conduct its search, and 3. supplements the firm's objectives
with decision rules which narrow the firm's selection process to
the most attractive opportunities.

Next, the question is raised whether, and under what conditions, a firm needs to have a strategy. In the third section an
answer is provided which relates the type of preferred strategy to
the type of firm.

Definitions of strategy found in business literature are different
from ours and are sometimes used interchangeably with the term

'policy'. The last section compares these definitions and relates them to different degrees of uncertainty under which business decisions are made.

CONCEPT OF THE FIRM'S BUSINESS AND THE COMMON THREAD

Objectives set the performance levels which a firm seeks to achieve, but they do not describe the business of the firm, unless statements such as 'the firm is in 20 per cent ROI business' or in 'flexible position business' are constructed to provide the description. Levitt[76] has suggested that a more definitive description of the firm's role in the environment is requisite for growth and success. Such description should encompass a broad scope of natural extensions of the firm's product-market position, derived from some core characteristic of the present business. Thus railways would view themselves in the 'transportation business' and petroleum companies in the 'energy business'.

While plausible, such business concepts leave some unanswered questions. Does it follow from this concept that railways should be in the long-haul trucking industry? The answer would seem to be yes. But how about taxi-cab or rental car business? These are also transportation industries, but at first glance would seem to have little in common with railways. It is hard to see where the skills, facilities, and experience of railway companies have anything to contribute to the latter areas. Consider the energy business for petroleum companies. Does it follow that they should diversify into fabrication of uranium fuel for atomic power plants, build the power plants, or retail electricity? The respective management, technical, production, and marketing skills are all different. Where is the common core capability?

The weakness with concepts such as 'transportation business' or 'energy business' is that they are too broad and do not provide what the investment community calls a 'common thread' – a relationship between present and future product-markets which would enable outsiders to perceive where the firm is heading, and the inside management to give it guidance.

95

A separate question is how strong the common thread must be. Royal Little has built the successful Textron Corp. composed of consumer electronics, textiles, helicopters, work shoes, and satellite motors, etc. – all without a strongly apparent common thread. Peter Grace took his company from bananas and shipping into chemicals, also with apparent success. The Du Pont Company however, has built its great success by closely following a very clearly defined common thread.

In seeking to answer these questions it is useful to review how firms usually identify the nature of their business. Some firms are identified by the characteristics of their product line. Thus there are 'transistor companies', 'machine tool companies', and 'automobile companies'. Others are described by the technology which underlies the product line, such as 'steel companies', 'aluminium companies', and 'glass companies'. Each may sell a wide range of different products to different users, but a common thread is provided by a manufacturing and/or engineering technology.

Firms are also described in terms of their markets. Here it is useful to make a distinction between customers and missions. A *mission* is an existing product *need;* a *customer* is the actual *buyer* of the product: the economic unit (such as an individual, a family, a business firm) which possesses both the need and the money with which to satisfy it.

The usefulness of this distinction lies in the fact that sometimes the customer is erroneously identified as the common thread of a firm's business. In reality a given type of customer will frequently have a range of unrelated product missions or needs. He would not necessarily satisfy them through the same purchasing channels, nor use the same approach to buying. Thus, the individual consumer fills his food needs at the supermarket and his entertainment needs at a television dealer's. Since the product technology, the distribution channels, and the customer motivation are different, no strong common thread is available to a firm which would attempt to sell both food and television sets. Similarly, the U.S. Department of Defense is a customer for a very wide range of missions. A company which supplies weapon systems for combat missions of the Army would have a better common thread in supplying control systems to industry than in selling replacement parts for Army trucks.

In selecting a useful range of missions of a particular customer, a firm needs to find a common thread either in product characteristics, technology, or similarity of needs. Thus agricultural machinery firms supply a range of needs of the farmer. All of these are related parts of his overall mission of tilling and harvesting the soil. Similarly, a home appliance manufacturer offers effort-saving products for the home which may range from washing machines to electronic irons.

In this perspective it is easy to see why the term 'transportation business' fails to supply the common thread. First, the range of possible missions is very broad: intra-urban, inter-urban, intra-continental, and inter-continental transportation; through the media of land, air, water, underwater; for moving passengers, and/or cargo. Second, the range of customers is wide: the individual, family, business firm, or government office. Third, the 'product' varies: car, bus, train, ship, aeroplane, helicopter, taxi, truck. The number of practical combinations of the variables is large, and so is the number of common threads.

While such a concept of business is too broad to be useful, the traditional identification of a firm with a particular industry has become too narrow. Today a great many firms find themselves in a number of different industries. Furthermore, the boundaries of industries are continually changing, and new ones are being born. For example, radio, television, transistor, home appliance, and atomic energy are all industries which did not exist fifty years ago. The need is for a concept of business which on the one hand will give specific guidance for the firm and on the other hand will provide room for growth. We shall describe such a concept in the next section.

COMPONENTS OF STRATEGY

To the extent the respective objectives and goals are consonant with actual performance, they do provide an indirect description of a common thread. Thus, a firm which has shown a consistent

97

rate of high growth is usually recognized by the investment community as a 'growth firm', and a well-diversified one as a 'broadly based' firm. Both of these descriptions can be constructively used by management as guidance in selecting new product-market areas.

However, this guidance is very weak and assures no common thread within the firm. Thus a 'growth' firm may be simultaneously in pharmaceutics, banking, and industrial controls – areas which have no relationship to one another, except that they may all have attractive growth prospects.

A somewhat more positive specification of the common thread is arrived at through the use of the *product-market scope*. This specifies the particular industries to which the firm confines its product-market position and it has the advantage of focusing search on well-defined areas for which common statistics and economic forecasts are generally available. However, many industries offer a range of products, missions, technologies, and customers which is so broad as to make the common thread very tenuous. For example, the electronics industry ranges from high growth in technologically sophisticated areas, such as optical electronics, to slow-growth consumer oriented product-markets, such as radio and television. To convey a common thread, description of the product-market scope frequently needs to be made in terms of sub-industries which contain product-markets and technologies with similar characteristics.

Another useful specification of common thread is through the means of the *growth vector*, which indicates the direction in which the firm is moving with respect to its current product-market posture. This can be illustrated by means of a matrix shown in Table 6.1. *Market penetration* denotes a growth direction through the increase of market share for the present product-markets. In *market development* new missions are sought for the firm's products. *Product development* creates new products to replace current ones. Finally, *diversification* is distinctive in the fact that both products and missions are new to the firm. The common thread is clearly indicated, in the first three alternatives, to be either the marketing skills or product technology or both. In diversification the common thread is less apparent and is certainly weaker.

Specification of the common thread through the growth vector is complementary to the product-market scope, since it gives the directions *within* an industry as well as *across* industry boundaries which the firm proposes to pursue. As we shall see in the next chapter, it is a very useful tool in arriving at the basic diversification decisions.

A third way to see a common thread is to isolate characteristics of unique opportunities within the field defined by the product-market scope and the growth vector. This is the *competitive advantage*. It seeks to identify particular properties of individual product-markets which will give the firm a strong competitive

TABLE 6.1 *Growth Vector Components*

Product Mission	Present	New
Present	Market penetration	Product development
New	Market development	Diversification

position. Thus, a firm might seek acquisitions which are large enough to give it a commanding position in the new industry. Or it might insist on entries which enjoy strong patent protection. Or it might consider only 'breakthrough' products which make obsolete previously available products (just as the electric typewriter made the manual one obsolete and was in turn made obsolete by the IBM rotary head machine).

The triplet of specifications – the product-market scope, the growth vector, and the competitive advantage – describes the firm's product-market path in the *external environment*. The first describes the scope of search, the second the directions within the scope, and the third the characteristics of individual entries.

99

There remains one other alternative for describing the common thread, and that is *synergy*. As described in a preceding chapter, synergy is a measure of the firm's ability to make good on a new product-market entry. The common thread may be *aggressive*, requiring that new entries make use of an outstanding competence possessed by the firm (say, a nationwide chain of retail outlets or leadership in computer technology), or it may be *defensive*, requiring that new entries supply some key competence which the firm lacks. It may, of course, be both aggressive and defensive. Synergy is especially useful as the common thread in new growth areas where industry boundaries are ill-defined and changing. It is also a key variable in the choice of a diversification strategy.

The classification of common thread into product-market scope, growth vector, competitive advantage, and synergy is given added meaning when viewed in the light of the firm's search for profitability. The first triplet of specifications describes the firm's search for *inherently* profitable opportunities in the external environment. The first sets the scope for the search, the second the directions within the scope, and the third the characteristics of outstanding opportunities. The firm may not realize the full profitability potential or may even lose money unless it has the capabilities required for success in the new ventures. This is provided by the fourth criterion, synergy.

The four characteristics are thus complementary, rather than mutually exclusive. We will call them, therefore, the *components of strategy*.* In conjunction with its objectives the firm may choose one, two, or all of the strategy components. For example, a chemical firm may specify the following:

1. OBJECTIVES: ROI: Threshold 10 per cent, goal 15 per cent
   SALES GROWTH RATE: Threshold 5 per cent, goal 10 per cent

2. STRATEGY
   a. Product-market scope: Basic chemicals and pharmaceuticals.
   b. Growth vector: Product development and concentric† diversification.

* In Chapter 9 we shall add another component: the 'make or buy'.
† This term will be defined in the next chapter.

c. Competitive advantage: Patent protection, superior research competence.

d. Synergy: Use of the firm's research capabilities and production technology.

Thus strategy and objectives together describe the concept of the firm's business. They specify the amount of growth, the area of growth, the directions for growth, the leading strengths, and the profitability target. Furthermore, they are now stated operationally: in a form usable for guiding management decisions and actions.*

IS STRATEGY NECESSARY?

To define strategy is not to prove that it is necessary for each firm. The question of the usefulness of strategy as a management tool must, therefore, be examined. We will do this by first examining the alternative to strategy. This alternative is to have no rules beyond the simple decision to look for profitable prospects.†
Under these conditions the firm does not select formal objectives, performs no appraisals, formulates no search and evaluation rules. Instead, it would inform the business world, as did Socony Mobil Company, of its interest in 'good' profitable opportunities; it would evaluate each new opportunity on the merits of its individual profitability.

Several reasons can be given in favour of this approach.

1. The firm would save the time, money, and executive talent which are required for a thorough strategic analysis. It will become evident in the following chapters that such savings can be very considerable.

2. The field of potential opportunities will be in no way restricted. Objectives and strategy limit the field of its search. Since

---

* A different and interesting classification of business strategies has been devised by L. C. Sorrell.[77] Among his strategies are the following: 'strike while the iron is hot', 'time is a great healer', 'bore from within', 'in union there is strength', 'draw a red herring across the trail', 'pass the buck', and 'conserve your gunpowder'.

† Example: Comment on diversification attributed to a vice-president of Socony Mobil's Center Division: 'We'll find money to invest in any proposal that shows promise of a substantial return.'[78]

strategy is based on uncertain and incomplete knowledge, there is a chance that some attractive opportunities will be missed. An opportunistic firm takes no such chances.

3. The firm reaps the full advantage of the 'delay principle'. By delaying commitment until an opportunity is in hand, it is able to act on the basis of the best possible information.

Counterposed to these are some weighty disadvantages.

1. In the absence of strategy, there are no rules to guide the search for new opportunities, both inside and outside the firm. Internally, the research and development department has no guidelines for its contribution to diversification. The external acquisition department similarly lacks focus. Thus the firm as a whole either passively waits for opportunities, or pursues a 'buckshot' search technique.

2. Project decisions will be of poorer quality than in firms with strategy. Without a focus for its efforts, the staff will lack the depth of knowledge in any particular area needed for competent analysis. Without strategy criteria, it will lack tools for recognizing outstanding opportunities. As a result managers acting on such advice will be forced into extreme forms of behaviour. Conservatives will refuse to take what under better information might be reasonable risks; entrepreneurs will plunge without appreciation of potential costs and dangers.

3. The firm will have no formal provision for partial ignorance. No yardsticks will be available to judge whether a particular opportunity is a rare one, or whether much better ones are likely to develop in the future. Thus there will be a danger of either premature over-commitment of resources or of failure fully to utilize the resources available within a budget period.

4. Without the benefit of a periodic appraisal, the firm would have no assurance that its overall resource allocation pattern is efficient and that some product lines are not obsolete.

5. The firm will lack an internal ability to anticipate change. Without a strategy, managers will either do nothing or risk the danger of acting at cross-purposes. For example, the director of marketing could assume that the growth will be attained through adding new products to the existing product line. He will proceed to expand and strengthen the present marketing organization. At

the same time, the director of engineering could assume that progress is to be made by eliminating the obsolete product line and diversifying into brand-new markets. He would, therefore, take appropriate action to curtail support of existing products and initiate developments for radically new missions. The potential result would be a marketing organization with no products to sell and a product line without a marketing capability.

To summarize, the advantages of not missing any bets and of not committing the firm's resources until the last moment are pitted against the disadvantages of inefficient search, enhanced risk of making bad decisions, and lack of control over the overall resource-allocation pattern.

It would seem that for most firms the advantages of strategy will outweigh those of total flexibility. However, strategy requirements will differ from one type of firm to another.

1. A type of firm which needs the most comprehensive strategy is a fully integrated operating firm. Since its product-market decisions have long lead times, it needs guidance for R & D, and it must be able to anticipate change. Much of its investment is irreversible, since it goes into R & D, which cannot be recovered, and physical assets, which are difficult to sell. It must, therefore, minimize the chances of making bad decisions.

2. A holding company has less stringent strategy requirements. It does not seek synergy among it subsidiaries, nor does it use internal R & D as a primary source for diversification. Each subsidiary operates independently, and the common thread among them is primarily financial. The holding company does need objectives with threshold-goals type of provisions for partial ignorance. Its strategy would have no synergy component or growth vector component. It would include a component of competitive advantage, since it naturally prefers good, rather than average, acquisitions. Such a firm may or may not have a well-defined product-market scope to help focus search and develop local expert knowledge of some industries. If present, the scope will reduce the chance of making bad acquisitions. However, some holding firms prefer to take the chance in favour of fully flexible choice. Although potentially costly, divestment from undesirable subsidiaries is feasible and widely practiced.

3. At the other extreme from a fully integrated firm is a company which primarily buys and sells. This may be an investment trust, a pension fund, or a real estate syndicate. Its position differs from the holding company in that the 'portfolio' of holdings is widely diversified and is highly negotiable, and the transfer costs are relatively low (sales tax, commission fees, etc.). Because portfolios are widely diversified, such firms seldom have the depth of knowledge of individual industries to enable them to seek a specific competitive advantage. Their strategy-formulation requirements are usually confined to objectives which are established on the basis of generally available industry data. Thus, for example, investment funds choose between the role of a 'growth fund' and that of a 'current earnings fund'.

The three types of company above were described in what might be called 'pure form'. In actuality there are various shadings of characteristics which make it difficult to place firms into one of the slots. There are different degrees of integration in operating companies, some companies act as holding firms in some respects and operating in others, and some investment firms *do* have industry experts and *do* specialize in certain industries. Therefore, each individual firm will have to determine its strategy requirement using the classification as a guide. The following summary table may be useful for this purpose.

It can easily be seen from the table that the operating firm requires the most complex strategy.* The remainder of the development will continue to deal with the more complex case.

STRATEGY, POLICY, PROGRAMMES, AND OPERATING PROCEDURES

The concept of strategy is relatively new to management literature. Its historical origin lies in the military art, where it is a broad, rather vaguely defined, 'grand' concept of a military campaign for *application* of large-scale forces against an enemy. Strategy is

---

* Investment funds which trade in listed securities have the additional advantage of knowing the full field of choice. There is no partial ignorance. This and low transfer costs permit an approach to the strategic problem which is much simpler than the present method.[79]

TABLE 6.2 *Strategy Requirements for Different Firms*

Type of firm \ Strategy requirement	P–M scope	Growth vector	Synergy	Competitive advantage	Objectives
Operating firm	✓	✓	✓	✓	✓
Holding company	✓(?)			✓	✓
Investment company					✓

contrasted to *tactics*, which is a specific scheme for *employment* of allocated resources.

The bridge to business usage was provided in 1948 by Von Neumann and Morgenstern[80] in their now-famous theory of games. The theory provides a unifying viewpoint for all types of conflict situations, regardless of whether their origin is in war, politics, or business. The concept of strategy is given two meanings. A *pure* strategy is a move or a specific series of moves by a firm, such as a product development programme in which successive products and markets are clearly delineated. A *grand* or *mixed* strategy is a statistical decision rule for deciding which particular pure strategy the firm should select in a particular situation.

Although game theory has not resulted in many practical applications, it has revolutionized ways of thinking about social problems in general and business in particular. One of the consequences was the increasing use of the concept of strategy in business literature. As one would expect, some business writers borrowed from game theory to define strategy as a set of specific product-market entries,[81] while others have defined it in the military sense as the broad overall concept of the firm's business.[82] In the latter sense strategy is often used interchangeably * with, or

* As for example in 'Strategy of Product Policy'.[83]

instead of, the term *policy*, which has long been a standard part of familiar business vocabulary.

In the business vocabulary, policy is also widely used in a very different sense in manuals of organization and procedures to denote a specific response to specific repetitive situations, e.g. 'overtime reimbursement policy', 'foul weather policy', 'educational refund policy', policy for the evaluation of inventories. A contingent event is recognized, such as a periodic need to work overtime, or a snowstorm. What needs to be done and the outcomes of such contingencies are *well known*; the contingencies are repetitive, but the time of specific occurrences cannot be specified in advance. In view of this, it is not worth while to require a new decision on what should be done each time overtime is needed or each time it snows. A better and more economical procedure is to prescribe, in advance, the response to be made whenever a specified contingency occurs. This is done through a written statement of the appropriate policy and of accompanying procedures for its implementation. Since the management decision is thus made in advance of the event, a rule for behaviour can be imposed on lower levels of supervision. Thus economies of management are realized, and consistency of action is assured.

When compared with our definition of strategy this meaning of policy is seen to be distinct and different. Policy is a *contingent decision*, where strategy is a *rule for making decisions*. Thus while implementation of policy can be delegated downward, implementation of strategy cannot, since last-minute executive judgement will be required. In technical terms, used by mathematical decision theorists, specification of strategy is forced under conditions of *partial ignorance*, when alternatives cannot be arranged and examined in advance, whereas under conditions of *risk* (alternatives are all known and so are their probabilities) or *uncertainty* (alternatives are known but not the probabilities), the consequences of different alternatives *can* be analysed in advance and decision made contingent on their occurrence. The lower level executive merely needs to recognize the event and then act in accordance with his instructions.

As mentioned previously, condition of risk may mean assignment of probability either to the *occurrence* of an event or to its possible *outcomes*. When the occurrence is certain, but the outcome is either certain or uncertain, a different kind of decision, called a *programme*, is possible; this is a time-phased action sequence used to guide and coordinate operations. When the occurrence of an alternative is not only certain but also repetitive, the decision takes the form of a *standing operating procedure*.

Thus, the several types of decisions commonly made within a firm can be ranked in the order of increasing level of ignorance: standing operating procedures and programmes under conditions of certainty or partial risk, policies under conditions of risk and uncertainty, and strategies under conditions of partial ignorance.

There is an unfortunate coincidence in our definitions. We speak of 'strategic' decisions,* where 'strategic' means 'relating to firm's match to its environment', and of 'strategy', where the word means 'rules for decision under partial ignorance'. This coincidence should not obscure the fact that all four basic types of decision described above – strategy, policy, programme, and standing operating procedure – occur in all three classes of problems: strategic, administrative, and operating. However, since conditions of partial ignorance are dominant in the strategic, but not the other two problems, the use of similar terminology is not entirely inappropriate.

It should further be made clear that all of the basic types of decisions may apply on organizational levels below the firm as a whole. Thus, for example, functional organizations, such as research, development, finance, and marketing, have a strong interface with the outside environment and will frequently be faced with conditions of partial ignorance. Under these conditions they will require appropriate strategies, such as R & D strategy, finance strategy, marketing strategy.

* Perhaps a better term would have been *entrepreneurial*.

CHAPTER 7

Why Firms Diversify

> I don't know of any more difficult management problem than
> that of diversifying . . . while diversification is fine as a matter
> of abstract principle, it can result in so many different eggs in one
> basket that nothing really significant is hatched out of any of
> them.
>
> JOSEPH T. WRIGHT

THE PROBLEM

IT was pointed out in Chapter 1 that a firm's concern with the
strategic problem is not automatic and that, in the absence of a
trigger signal, most managements will focus their attention on
administrative and operating decisions. In the first section of this
chapter we explore alternative conditions for the trigger signal
and suggest an approach to initiating a strategic analysis.

A milestone in this analysis is arrived at when the firm faces
the decision whether or not to diversify. The second section
explores conditions under which diversification is indicated and
relates the decision to management attitudes toward risk.

The third section explores alternative directions for diversification and relates these to the objectives of the firm. The pros and
cons of a popular form, the conglomerate diversification, are
explored.

THE TRIGGER SIGNAL

In Chapter 1 we called attention to the fact that, unlike operating
and administrative decisions, strategic decisions are not self-
regenerative. Attention to strategy is either assured on a continual basis through special organizational arrangements, or it
remains dormant until triggered off by some major event inside or
outside the firm.

Until the early 1920s there appears to have been no understanding of organizational implications of strategy. Therefore,
concern with strategy had followed an 'on–off' cycle attuned to

the appearance of major strategic opportunities, which were called 'new business frontiers'. Chandler[84] traces the history of several such cycles during which broadening of product-market horizons alternated with periods of preoccupation with operating and administrative problems created by strategic change. He further records that the changeover points frequently coincided with changes from one generation of management to another; far-sighted outward oriented entrepreneurs of the expansion era gave way to methodical profit-minded efficiency experts. A dramatic example is provided by the change within General Motors from the Durant to the Sloan Era.[85]

In the early 1920s, for quite different reasons, Du Pont and General Motors pioneered in the introduction of a new organizational concept. A layer of management was created in these firms divorced from operating responsibilities and charged with formulation of policy and strategy, planning, and performance appraisal. Since product-market strategy was only one of the major responsibilities of these managers, and since, as was suggested in Chapter 1, operating and administrative concerns tend to pre-empt the strategic, the new organizational concept encouraged, but did not guarantee, analysis of product-market strategy.* As a result, continual attention to strategy has remained dependent not only on organizational structure but also on the orientation of the management. Some firms, such as Litton, General Dynamics (during the Hopkins regime) and Textron (during Roya-Little's) made strategic change a way of life. Others, such as Underwood and Baldwin Lima Hamilton, for a long time remained impervious to their respective grave strategic problems. Many large firms followed the GM–Du Pont organizational pattern, but their newly promoted policy makers had not been able to break away from their former jobs of running the company.[87]

* As a matter of fact, it appears that, while Du Pont's reorganization was heavily influenced by product-market problems, General Motors initially took the step to resolve a number of very pressing operating and administrative problems. Later on, as Sloan's book shows, he used his powerful position to force explicit formulation of product-market strategy within GM.[86]

For firms which have no provisions for response to strategic challenges and which refuse to anticipate it, the awareness of the problem usually comes through a traumatic experience, such as a drastic drop in sales or earnings, a product breakthrough by competition, a continued failure to meet profit objectives or a 'sweep of the new broom' triggered by change in top management. The unfortunate fact about this route is that the challenge often comes at a time when the firm is ill-prepared to cope with it. Nor is it an easy challenge to meet, because, as discussed in Chapter 1, the symptoms are usually ambiguous. Considerable analysis is required to arrive at a conclusion that the problem is, in fact, strategic; at the same time the tendency is to seek solutions in operating (cost reduction!) and administrative (reorganization!) changes.

There is considerable evidence to suggest that many firms can no longer treat strategic change as a one-time response, put the product-market posture in order, and then revert to operating and administrative concerns. The post-World War II deluge of technology, the dynamism of the world-wide changes in market structure, and the saturation of demand in many major United States industries all have contributed to a drastic shortening of the strategy–operations-strategy cycle which management used to follow according to Chandler. It appears, in fact, that in many industries, such as electronics, chemicals, pharmaceuticals, plastics, and aerospace, there is no longer any cycle. Strategic change is so rapid that firms must continually survey the product-market environment in search for diversification opportunities.*

The preceding suggests that:

1. In the present business environment, no firm can consider itself immune to threats of product obsolescence and saturation of demand.

2. In some industries, surveillance of the environment for strategic threats and opportunities needs to be a continuous process.

* This increased pace is illustrated by the current rate of merger and acquisition activity, which is one of the major instruments of strategic change. The post-World War II decade has been described as the third great major wave in American business history.[88]

3. As a minimum, firms in all industries need to make regular periodic reviews of product-market strategy.

The key question, therefore, is not whether to direct management attentions to strategy, but rather how and to what extent. For a firm which faces it for the first time, this question has a chicken and egg quality; a definitive answer cannot be given until a first complete analysis has been carried out along the lines which will be discussed in the succeeding pages. However, certain preliminary guidelines for decision can be set down.

1. Clearly, the intensiveness of the analysis will be limited by the resources of the firm. A one-man top management will of necessity be forced into a highly condensed review of strategy; a large multi-divisional firm can afford a thorough study.

2. The characteristics of the firm's product-market environments will have a dominant influence.

a. If the industry is highly dynamic, change in technology rapid, and/or market structure unstable, the firm will need to put strategic change on a permanent basis. It might as well face this need at the outset, even before the first analysis is undertaken.

b. If, on the other hand, the industry is one of the few remaining ones which have enjoyed relative stability in the past, it is best to wait until the first results are in before deciding on administrative changes. In such cases the firm may be well advised to secure competent outside help for the initial analysis.

3. The magnitude of the needed product-market realignment will influence the decision. If the problem appears as a minor 'soft spot' in an otherwise healthy product-market position, temporary *ad hoc* arrangement for correcting it may suffice. If a wholesale revision of the position appears necessary, a major allocation of resources on a long-term semi-permanent basis is indicated.

If the final conclusion is that a major effort is required on the strategic problem, far-reaching organizational changes will probably have to follow. It is important to recognize that traditional organizational forms have evolved for the primary pursuit of the operating problem. Adoption of Du Pont–General Motors

111

concept does not guarantee that strategy will be attended to.*
The costs and the risks attendant on strategic change require that
top executive talent be given full-time responsibility for the effort
and that it be supported with adequate staff resources and budgets.

This issue becomes particularly acute in a small firm where all
kinds of 'indirect' staff expense have traditionally been viewed as
wasteful and to be avoided at all cost.† Our discussion suggests
that if the firm is in a highly dynamic environment, it will obtain
better growth and profitability if part of the total budget is used to
support a small staff created for the purpose of searching out
new products and markets, performing exploratory market
research, and evaluating opportunities.

WHY FIRMS DIVERSIFY

Strategic change, as we have defined it, is a realignment of the
firm's product-market environment. This does not necessarily
mean diversification, as shown in the revised growth vector
matrix below. The growth is now in two parts, expansion and
diversification. It will be recalled from Chapter 4 that the former
consists of market penetration, market development, and product
development.

In this perspective, it would be incorrect to say that most firms
neglect the strategic problem between major crises. On the contrary, a majority seeks to improve its product and process technology, expand sales territory, and increase share of the market.
In most cases these are natural and routine extensions of the
present product-market position brought about by extrapolation
of trends in R&D, perceived changes in customer demand, and
availability of new materials. Thus it is fair to say that in most
firms strategy does not remain static but evolves, however slowly,
in response to changes in environment. Until recently this process
has remained largely unplanned.

* Both Chandler's book and common experience show that in many firms
newly created top-level policy makers continue to run rather than plan the
company.

† Hence the traditional practice of using the indirect to direct personnel
ratio as a major yardstick of management efficiency.

While much needs to be said about planning the evolutionary development, our concern in this book is primarily with major changes in the product-market orientation. As the preceding matrix suggests this change can be brought about through a major revision in the expansion strategy and/or through diversification. By its very definition diversification is the more drastic and risky of the two strategies, since it involves a simultaneous departure from familiar products and familiar markets. The deci-

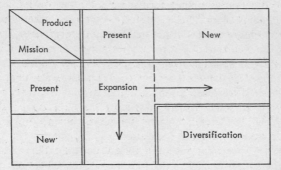

Figure 7.1. Product-mission matrix.

sion on whether or not to diversify represents a major milestone in a firm's development. Therefore, it will be useful to explore reasons why firms diversify.

A number of papers are available in management literature which list many different reasons for diversification.[89] These can be reduced to a few underlying reasons.

1. *Firms diversify when their objectives can no longer be met within the product-market scope defined by expansion.*

In the area of proximate and long-term profitability objectives the cause may be market saturation, general decline in demand, competitive pressures, or product-line obsolescence. A typical symptom is a drop in the rate of return on reinvestments into the present business; another is a 'drying up' of the stream of new opportunities.

In the area of the flexibility objective, the cause may be a disproportionately large fraction of sales to a single customer, a

113

generally narrow market or technological base, or influx of new technologies into the firm's product-market scope.

2. Even if attractive expansion opportunities are still available and past objectives are being met, *a firm may diversify, because the retained cash exceeds the total expansion needs.* The rate of return available on liquid resources (from banks, bonds, etc.) is generally lower than that from operations. The pressure may be on the firm to invest the money more profitably.* We say 'may' because many conservative managements prefer not to diversify under these circumstances. This is attested to by a very large number of firms which are currently in a highly liquid position.[90]

3. Even if current objectives are being met, *a firm may diversify when diversification opportunities promise greater profitability than expansion opportunities.* This may occur under several conditions.

a. When diversification opportunities are sufficiently attractive to offset their inherently lower synergy.

b. When the firm's research and development organization produces outstanding diversification by-products.

c. When synergy is not an important consideration and hence the synergy advantages of expansion over diversification are not important. This is true, for example, in an investment firm which deals in securities.

4. *Firms may continue to explore diversification when the available information is not reliable enough to permit a conclusive comparison between expansion and diversification.* This situation occurs quite frequently, since a firm normally has a great deal more information about expansion prospects than about the vast outside field of diversification.

In such situations many firms have shown in the recent past an unfortunate tendency to plunge rather than probe.† A much

---

* Under these conditions an alternative to diversification is to distribute excess equity among the stockholders. A comparison of these alternatives is beyond the scope of this book.

† This is attested to by numerous histories of disappointments during the last two merger waves,[88] and by the fact that many firms are now seeking diversification through the medium of one- or two-man departments, where hundreds or even thousands are employed in pursuing relatively less risky expansion moves.

less costly long-run approach is to buy reliable information before buying diversification.

The above list points to some significant conclusions. As was suggested in Chapter 3, the goals of the firm are not absolute, but are closely related to opportunities. Under reasons 2. and 3. above, firms would pursue diversification when an opportunity to revise the goals upward presents itself. Under reason 1., if analysis of opportunities shows that diversification cannot improve the firm's position, the goals will have to be revised downward.

This absence of an absolute 'proper' set of goals for a firm gives the management great latitude in exercising its risk preferences. Conservative managers would be content to limit interest in diversification to reason 1. Thus if the firm does meet its current objective, diversification will not be pursued. This attitude is not uncommon among top managers who are operations minded and whose training and experience has been confined to a single industry.

On the other hand, entrepreneurially oriented managers would view the firm as a pattern of investments to be amended and changed when better opportunities arise. They would consider all four reasons as appropriate to diversification activity.

These differences of attitude will obviously have a major influence on the decision to diversify or not. Therefore, in the following analysis of this decision we shall provide for both attitudes.

DIVERSIFICATION ALTERNATIVES

In the preceding section we had divided the growth direction vector into an expansion and a diversification component. Each can be further expanded in terms of characteristics of products and customers in relation to the present product-market position. Such expansion is shown in Figure 7.2 for the diversification component. The product alternatives are divided into those which are related to the present technological base and those which are technologically new to the firm. The missions are sub-divided according to types of customers. The names of the various types of diversification alternatives are common in business literature.[91]

To give some meaning in practice to the respective classifications, we have prepared a sample table of growth vector alternatives for an automobile manufacturer. This is shown in Figure 7.3.

An important characteristic of horizontal diversification is that it consists of moves *within* the economic environment of the diversifying firm. Therefore, those industries which happen to contribute horizontal opportunities will usually rank low on

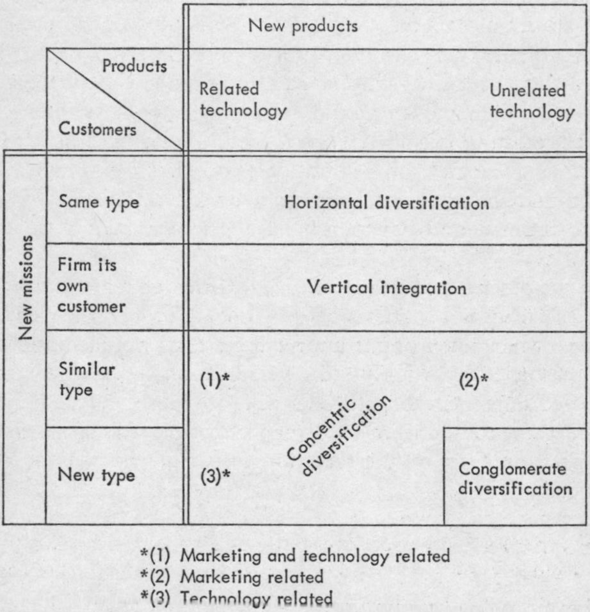
New products
Products
Customers
Related technology
Unrelated technology
New missions
Same type
Horizontal diversification
Firm its own customer
Vertical integration
Similar type
(1)*
(2)*
Concentric diversification
New type
(3)*
Conglomerate diversification
*(1) Marketing and technology related
*(2) Marketing related
*(3) Technology related

Figure 7.2. Growth vectors in diversification.

flexibility and will contribute little toward improvement of stability of the firm. The strong common thread in this type of diversification is found in marketing synergy, since the firm continues to sell through established marketing channels.

Vertical integration is even more sensitive to instabilities and will offer less assurance of flexibility. In fact, by putting more eggs into the same end-product basket, vertical integration increases the firm's dependence on a particular segment of economic demand. Synergy will be strong if technology is related, but may actually be quite weak, and even negative, in the case of related technology. This occurs because the management practices and technology in producing parts or materials for the present products are often very different from those of the firm. If the new operation is closely controlled by the parent and integrated into the parent organization, dis-economies may occur, and inappro-

Product / Customer	Related technology	Unrelated technology
Same type	Motorcyles, lawnmowers, intra-urban personal vehicles	Electric home appliances
Firm its own customer	Gas turbine engines wheels transmissions	Paint, glass, tires, etc.
Similar type	Farm tractors and machinery	Computers for small business
New type	Diesel locomotives Missile ground support equipment	Petrochemicals drugs

Figure 7.3. Sample growth vectors for an automobile manufacturer.

priate management decisions may be made. This danger is aggravated if the parent cannot absorb all of the subsidiary's output and must learn new marketing techniques by selling to his own competitors! The history of vertical integration by Henry Ford, Sr and subsequent partial 'dis-integration' by the firm offers an example of many of these problems.

Thus both vertical and horizontal diversification vectors offer only a limited potential for objectives. They make a limited contribution to flexibility and stability and they will contribute to the other objectives only if the present economic environment of the firm is healthy and growing.

The remaining two directions – concentric and conglomerate

diversification – differ in the degree of synergy with the firm's present position. Although more tenuous than in other vectors, concentric diversification has a measure of common thread with the firm either through marketing or technology or both. Conglomerate diversification, by definition, has none. Both have the potential for meeting all of the objectives of the firm; however, a concentric strategy which matches a conglomerate strategy on economic prospects and on flexibility will usually be more profitable and less risky, because of synergy.

Thus, at first glance one would expect the concentric strategy to be preferred by an overwhelming majority of firms. In point of fact, however, the record shows the opposite; a great many appear to follow the conglomerate path. Several reasons can be offered for this.

1. There are many cases where firms have no strategy beyond a desire for profitable opportunities.* Seen from the outside they appear to follow a conglomerate strategy, whereas in fact they are 'marching in all directions'.†

2. The capabilities of some firms are too highly specialized or too obsolete to have synergy with other kinds of business. The former appears to be the cause in the search by missile-space companies for compatible diversification opportunities outside the defence industry.

3. In some firms the depth of competence is too shallow to offer opportunities for synergy, so that all diversification moves are conglomerate in nature.

* The difference between a conglomerate strategy and no strategy at all is that while the former has no synergy component, it will usually have a product-market scope, a competitive advantage component, as well as a set of clearly stated objectives.

† There is evidence that disappointing experience sometimes drives such firms toward a concentric approach. This appears to have been the case when American Machine and Foundry divested itself from ill-fated ventures into rocket propulsion and missile ground support equipment. This was certainly the case when General Mills recently made the following announcement: 'General Mills Inc. believes its abandonment of a wide diversification policy a year ago is proving worthwhile and the company intends to place emphasis on consumer foods and specialty chemical fields, General Rawlings, President, said at the annual meeting of stockholders . . .'[92]

4. In some firms the management's preference and training structure dispose it toward conglomerate growth.

The investment community appears to have been critical of the absence of an apparent common thread in conglomerate diversification and has tended to offer relatively low price/earnings multiples for such firms. In addition to lack of joint advantage, the objection seems to be that an outside investor has no sense of direction in which the firm is heading and hence would not feel secure for the future of his investment.

While this is certainly true of firms which have no strategy at all, it should be recognized that a well-formulated conglomerate strategy does have a sense of direction expressed through competitive advantage, product-market scope, and objectives, albeit less definite than in the concentric case, and that many firms have been successful in building up an impressive record of performance via the conglomerate route. For example, though it has not been widely publicized, Textron's conglomerate strategy had very definite criteria of competitive advantage, cost of entry, and earnings prospects which were applied to selection of acquisitions. By following this strategy the firm has built a good record of growth and earnings.

Since many firms will continue to use the conglomerate path and particularly since the distinction between concentric and conglomerate diversification is one of degree, it is useful to set forth the advantages and limitations of a purely conglomerate diversification strategy.

1. Conglomerate strategy can improve the overall profitability and flexibility of the firm through acquisition in industries which have better economic characteristics than those of the acquiring firm.

2. Although the consolidated performance may improve the firm's position, firms which pursue a conglomerate strategy into growth fields frequently dilute the earnings of their stockholders. Since the firm has no trading advantage it will generally pay the same discount for future earnings as the individual investors. This effect has been amply in evidence during the fifties in the many acquisitions into electronics.

3. In the absence of synergy, the combined operating

performance of a conglomerate firm will in general be no better than it would have been if the divisions operated as independent firms. The conglomerate firm will therefore have no operating competitive advantage (e.g. in terms of lower operating costs) over independents.

4. A conglomerate firm does have a potential advantage of better access to capital markets and better stability of earnings under normal conditions.

5. However, there is evidence [93] that under abnormal conditions, such as a recession, conglomerate firms have less staying power than concentric ones and hence suffer sharper reversals.

6. The inherent economic potential of a new industry must not be the sole criterion for conglomerate acquisitions. In addition, the acquiring firm should insist on a record of successful operation and evidence of competent management. The many abortive forays into 'promising situations' in electronics by a motley assortment of industries furnish strong support to the rule.

7. Organizational strategy is of great importance in conglomerate acquisitions. If internally well managed and left to themselves, divisions of a holding company should operate no worse than their independent competitors. However, if central management begins to assert decision prerogative other than financial, there is strong danger of negative synergy.

CHAPTER 8

The Appraisal

The Red Queen said, 'Now, *here*, it takes all the running *you* can do to keep in the same place. If you want to get somewhere else, you must run at least twice as fast as that!'

LEWIS CARROLL

THE PROBLEM

THUS far we have been concerned with development of basic concepts and tools for strategic analysis. The remainder of the book is devoted to using these in constructing a step-by-step solution of the strategic problem.

As discussed in Chapter 7, the expansion component of strategy offers strong transfer of product technology, or marketing competence, or both. In diversification, novel products are acquired and previously unexplored markets are entered. Therefore, given two otherwise equal opportunities, synergy will be higher in expansion than in diversification.* Consequently, the firm can expect higher profitability and lower risks from the former.

Put somewhat differently, this means that if a firm can meet all of its objectives by measures short of diversification, it should do so. This conclusion provides the logical structure to our approach to strategy formulation. Since diversification is costly and risky, the first section of this chapter (*internal appraisal*) is concerned with whether the firm can solve its problems without diversifying. If the problem cannot be solved within the limit of the present product-market position, presumption is strong that the firm has to diversify; if the conclusion is that the problem *can* be solved internally, the firm may or may not terminate the analysis, depending on the risk preferences of the management.

* This does not necessarily mean that synergy is altogether absent in diversification. On the contrary, we shall later use synergy as the primary variable in discussion of diversification strategy. However, the best synergy available through diversification will generally be lower than in comparable expansion moves.

121

In any case, a decision to continue analysis calls for a survey of opportunities outside the firm's present product-market scope (*external appraisal*). Comparison of the result with that of the internal appraisal leads to a final decision to diversify or not to diversify, and an allocation of the firm's resources among diversification on the one hand and expansion on the other.

A decision to diversify raises the question of whether the new acquisitions will be integrated into the firm's present organizational structure, or whether the structure will be varied so as to take advantage of the synergy potential. The choice of the *synergy-structure* relationship, discussed in the last section of this chapter, is a key management decision which affects the final product-market strategy of the firm.

It will soon become apparent that the flow of decisions leading to strategy formulation is complex, involves many contributing studies, and that it can be very time consuming. One such complete study of a firm consumed between five and seven man-years and cost between $100,000 and $200,000. Many firms, particularly smaller ones, may not be in a position to make such commitments. It will be helpful, therefore, if the following decision flow diagrams are interpreted according to circumstances of the reader. An executive of a small firm can treat them as guidelines for thinking through the strategic problem. He may not be able to afford many of the detailed studies, but he can, by using the diagrams as a road map and by making qualitative decisions, gain insight into the problems of his firm. On the other hand, management of larger firms can use the scheme as a related programme of studies to be contributed by responsible staff groups.

INTERNAL APPRAISAL

The decision flow diagram for an internal appraisal is shown graphically in Figure 8.1. In order to relate the diagram to the following discussion, numbers in brackets will be marked to correspond to appropriate boxes in the flow diagram.

As discussed earlier, strategic analysis may be typically triggered off by a signal of serious trouble or by a change in top management. Forward-looking management may anticipate

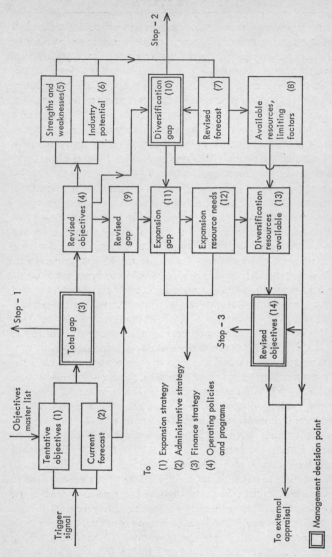

Figure 8.1. Decision flow in internal appraisal.

Objectives master list

Trigger signal

Tentative objectives (1)

Current forecast (2)

Total gap (3)

Stop – 1

Revised objectives (4)

Strengths and weaknesses (5)

Industry potential (6)

Stop – 2

Revised forecast (7)

Available resources, limiting factors (8)

Revised gap (9)

Diversification gap (10)

Expansion gap (11)

Expansion resource needs (12)

Diversification resources available (13)

Stop – 3

Revised objectives (14)

To external appraisal

To
(1) Expansion strategy
(2) Administrative strategy
(3) Finance strategy
(4) Operating policies and programs

☐ Management decision point

changes in the environment of the firm and act before difficulties arise. Aggressive management will make strategic change a way of life and periodically review its strategy regardless of performance.*

The first order of business will be preparation of *tentative objectives* (1). A firm new to strategic analysis may be faced with the problem of making its objectives explicit for the first time. Other firms will conduct a review of current objectives in the light of past performance and make a tentative revision in the priorities and the goals. The procedure for setting these objectives was described in Chapters 3 and 4.

Concurrently, a *current forecast* (2) of future performance will be made. This is constructed so as to predict the firm's performance on its high-priority objectives. If a long-range plan had been previously developed for the firm, it will serve as the foundation for the current forecast. The difference between the two will lie in the attributes for which the forecasts are made. Since long-range plans are usually confined to proximate profitability forecasts, additional information will have to be developed for the long-range (in our sense of the word) and flexibility objectives.

Firms which have no experience with long-range planning will find that a useful procedure is to start with the past history of performance, extrapolate this into the future, and then adjust it for factors which are expected to produce deviations from trends. The last step is particularly important, because many firms are addressing the strategic problem precisely because past trends have been broken by new developments.†

A comparison can now be made between objectives and the current forecast to measure the *total gap* (3) – the discrepancy between aspirations and anticipations. For example, a firm whose tentative objectives in the order of priority are 10 per cent ROI, 15 per cent growth rate, with one-half of the growth rate to come from new product-markets, may find that the forecast promises to meet the ROI goal but only a 12 per cent growth, and very little expectation of product-market innovation.

* For examples of the respective kind of management see Ref. 94.
† For one specific scheme see Ref. 95.

If such gap exists, *revised objectives* (4) are prepared. Clearly, if expectations exceed aspirations (a *negative* gap), objectives are adjusted upward. If the gap is positive, a different order of priority assignment to objectives may become apparent. In the above example increased priority is indicated for the flexibility objective. On other occasions the gap may be generally judged to be too great in the light of the trends and the limitations of the firm, and goal-threshold values are adjusted to lower acceptable values.

If, after these adjustments, a significant gap remains, the analysis moves to the next phase. If there is no gap, conservatively inclined management may choose to terminate analysis at this point until the next review date. Entrepreneurial management will choose to proceed with the purpose of discovering whether the firm can do even better than indicated by the current forecast. This optional management decision is indicated by an arrow and by the word 'STOP', appearing on Figure 8.1.

Throughout the study of the decision flow process we shall continue to indicate such management decision options at appropriate points in the analysis. It is necessary, therefore, to digress in order to make it clear that the term 'conservative' is in no sense meant to indicate a 'worse' choice, nor 'entrepreneurial' a 'better' one. We use these words to indicate different attitudes toward risk found among managers. By choosing a 'conservative' path, in our sense of the word, management chooses a combination of lower probable gain with a correspondingly lower risk than does an 'entrepreneur' who decides in favour of higher-gain–higher-risk course. Neither is inherently 'right' or 'wrong'.*

To return to the decision diagram, revision of objectives is followed by two concurrent analyses. The first, *strengths and weaknesses* (5), has already been discussed in Chapter 5. It will be recalled that it involves constructing a competence profile for the firm and comparing it with profiles of successful competitors to

---

* In mathematical decision theories 'indifference curves' are postulated which are intended to make comparable different gain-risk combinations. Unfortunately, no reliable data have been developed so far to make possible drawing of such curves for strategic business decisions.

develop a pattern of the firm's strengths and weaknesses relative to its present product-market strategy.

The other concurrent analysis is of the *industry potential* (6). Its purpose is to determine the growth potential available within the

TABLE 8.1 *Outline for Industry Analysis*

1. Product-Market Structure
   a. Products and their characteristics
   b. Product missions
   c. Customers
2. Growth and Profitability
   a. History
   b. Forecasts
   c. Relation to life cycle
   d. Basic determinants of demand
   e. Averages and norms typical of the industry
3. Technology
   a. Basic technologies
   b. History of innovation
   c. Technological trends – threats and opportunities
   d. Role of technology in success
4. Investment
   a. Cost of entry and exit-critical mass
   b. Typical asset patterns in firms
   c. Rate and type of obsolescence of assets
   d. Role of capital investment in success
5. Marketing
   a. Means and methods of selling
   b. Role of service and field support
   c. Role and means of advertising and sales promotion
   d. What makes a product competitive
   e. Role of marketing in success
6. Competition
   a. Market shares, concentration, dominance
   b. Characteristics of outstanding firms, of poor firms
   c. Trends in competitive patterns
7. Strategic Perspective
   a. Trends in demand
   b. Trends in product-market structure
   c. Trends in technology
   d. Key ingredients in success

industry to a firm which is willing and able to make an all-out effort to capitalize on it.

Rather than deal with extrapolations of the firm's performance, as was done in the current potential, industry potential explores the economic and competitive prospects for the industry as a whole. Trends in growth, profitability, and market shares are projected. The competitive environment is analysed from the viewpoint of the trend in demand to capacity and the cost of entry and exit from the industry. The technological trends and potential impact of new technologists are identified.

The various trends are put together into projections of performance which a fully competitive firm can attain along the principal attributes of our firm's objectives vector. In summarizing this analysis it is useful to interpret the data within the concept of the *industry life cycle*.* This concept is particularly helpful for avoiding the danger of linear projections of past trends. An outline which has been used for industry potential studies is shown in Table 8.1.

By combining the analyses of strengths and weaknesses with the industry potential and by referring to the current forecast, it is now possible to construct a new *revised forecast* (7) for the firm. This is done by assuming that, rather than continue in its present groove, the firm will make an all-out effort to take advantage of its opportunities, short of embarking on diversification. The analysis may show, for example, that the current forecast of return on investment is below the maximum expected potential. Further investigation may show this to be due primarily to the firm's traditional reluctance to shift from distributors to direct sales. This shift is feasible, and an assumption can be made that the firm can raise its ROI to or near the maximum possible. On the other hand, it may appear that the lag in profitability is to be ascribed to an unfortunate distribution of the firm's manufacturing plants and high attendant distribution costs. Although some improvements can be made, the basic pattern cannot be changed short of costly relocations. In this case a conclusion may be reached that the industry maximum is not attainable; the revised forecast will reflect this decision.

Preparation of the revised forecast will single out areas of strengths which the firm needs to exploit and measures to be remedied. These may be in the form of increases in operating

---

* For a discussion and use of the life-cycle concept see Ref. 96.

efficiency, changes in administrative arrangements (as in the example above) or in the product-market strategy, such as a shift of emphasis from seeking a large share of the market to intensified product development. These areas of action are earmarked for further analysis and implementation.

At this point, the analysis becomes somewhat less than straightforward. It will be recalled that the total gap (3) was determined

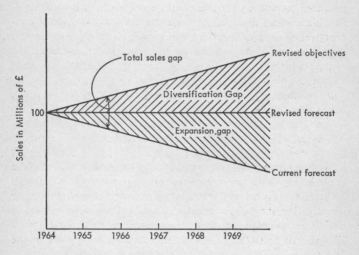

Figure 8.2. Breakdown of sales gap.

on the basis of tentative objectives (1) and that a new set of objectives was established (4). Therefore, the total gap needs to be revised. This is shown in box (9) – *revised total gap* – in which the current forecast is compared with the revised objectives. Next the revised forecast (7) is compared with the revised objectives to determine the *diversification gap* (10) which will remain after all internal steps have been implemented. The difference between this and the total gap is the *expansion gap* (11) which will be closed. To illustrate this still further Figure 8.2 shows how the respective gaps may look for the firm's sales potential. Similar graphs can be constructed for some other attributes of objectives. The two gaps thus show the respective contributions to be made from pursuing expansion and internal changes on the one hand, and diversification on the other.

Analysis of the gaps leads to another major management decision point. If the internal expansion measures promise to close the diversification gap, many firms will decide against diversification at this point in time. Again management risk preferences play an important role, but in a somewhat different way from the preceding decision point. As discussed earlier, a move from expansion to diversification entails, for some firms, not only greatly increased risks but also very high transfer costs. Such firms are usually highly integrated, with large fixed investments in physical assets and specialized business and technological know-how. They welcome an opportunity to redress imbalances in the present position without diversifying. On the other hand, firms with highly fluid and negotiable resources and without specialized know-how, such as an investment trust, would have no particular incentive to stop the analysis at this point. The incentive is rather to survey the broadest possible field of opportunities before selecting the product-market posture.

If, for any of the above reasons, the decision is to continue analysis, the next step is to determine the resources available to the firm for implementation of the respective changes. The revised forecast provides a basis for estimating the resources which will be generated (resources available (8)) for growth and expansion. The primary dimensions of this are the net *cash flow* which will be available above the operating needs and an estimate of *equity base* which will be available for acquisition activity. The latter is based on the present ownership patterns, the acceptable dilution of present ownership, and the acceptable dilution (if any) of earnings to present stockholders. The result is an estimate of the sterling value of equity available for trading. The usability of the equity for trading will depend on the firm's price/earnings position in relation to potential acquisitions. Resource analysis should single out the particular resources which may become *limiting factors* (8) in strategic activity. Quite frequently this will be competent general management, but it may also be a limited availability of raw materials, of skilled labour, or of middle management.*

Since the intent is to implement fully the expansion forecast before diverting resources to diversification, the next step is to make an estimate of *expansion requirements* (12). These are costs in terms of sterling, manpower, and other resources, over and above the operating costs, which are required to bring about expansion. They include expenditures on new and modernized facilities, administrative changes, and increases in advanced research activities.

The *diversification resources* (13) estimate is now obtained by comparing the total available resources (8) with the expansion requirements (12). It has to be recognized that diversification resources are self-regenerative, i.e. use of equity to acquire a firm may bring in a rich supply of ready cash for further expansion.† Therefore, the diversification resource is an estimate of capabilities for the *first phase* of the programme. Nevertheless, even with this reservation these resources may or may not be judged adequate for the diversification job required by the gap. Although accurate measurements of feasibility will not be possible until after outside opportunities are explored, major infeasibilities will be apparent at this stage. For example, if the flexibility objective requires that in five years 50 per cent of the firm's sales (or say $100 million per year) be in technologically fertile new product-markets, and the firm is short of cash and is selling at six to ten times earnings, the chances of the objective being met are very slim.‡

The last step in internal appraisal is another major decision point. The diversification gap is examined in relation to the diversification resources to determine whether the objectives need

* Limitations imposed by critical resources may or may not be recognized in the earlier strengths and weaknesses analysis. If a resource is already in short supply, it should appear as a weakness; but if it is just adequate for current operations, the limitation will not appear until later in the expansion or diversification programme.

† An excellent example of this strategy is described in Ref. 97.

‡ This example is based on an actual diversification history in which the infeasibility was not recognized.

another revision (14) and whether the firm should decide against diversification. It is possible that, as in the above example, there doesn't seem to be much chance of substantially narrowing the gap through diversification. In this case, the objectives may be revised downward to the level made possible by expansion only and a decision made not to diversify. It is also sometimes possible to change priorities of objectives to suit the resources. Thus, in the example the aggressive flexibility objective cannot be met, because firms with fertile technologies usually sell at a high times earnings multiple. However, revision of the objective to defensive flexibility would make certain unglamorous but steady industries acceptable to the firm, and firms in such industries *can* be acquired at six to ten times earnings.

In addition to gap size, the decision to proceed further will be influenced by the management risk-taking attitudes described in Chapter 7.

EXTERNAL APPRAISAL

The purpose of external appraisal is to analyse the product-market opportunities which are available to the firm outside its present scope and thus produce the final decision on whether the firm shall diversify. Theoretically (see Chapter 2) the process is quite simple. All opportunities are arrayed, each is tested for its contribution to the firm, and a group of top-ranking ones is selected for the diversification portfolio. As was discussed in Chapter 2, in practice this is a difficult task. A recapitulation of the major problems will help establish the logic for the external appraisal.

A major problem is posed by the fact that, instead of a single measurement, the purpose of the firm is described by a multi-dimensional vector of objectives. These objectives are measured in different units (they are not *commensurate*), and they compete for the firm's resources (they are not *colinear*). Thus, its proximate objective competes with the long-range ones, and the flexibility objectives compete with both.

Our approach to this problem will be straightforward. We shall use the respective objectives of the firm as criteria by which

131

opportunities are evaluated and ranked. This process will eliminate certain inefficient opportunities which are inferior to some other opportunities on all objectives. The remaining list will provide a basis for deciding whether external opportunities are attractive enough to justify diversification.

A second major problem is partial ignorance; at decision time we do not have the assurance that all of the forthcoming attractive opportunities have been identified and described. In previous chapters we sought to make provisions for partial ignorance through the goal-threshold concept. In external appraisal we shall deal with opportunities at the level of an industry (or a sub-industry), rather than with individual firms and products, precisely for the reason that at that level much data *are* available. These data, however, are usually in terms of averages for groups of firms and product-market areas. For example, data on the electronics component's industry will frequently average out the performance of conventional components, such as resistors, capacitors, and chokes, with exotic solid-state components and integrated circuity.

As a result of this aggregation, our perspective and decisions will lose the sharpness needed for selecting a particular firm or a particular product-market. This will be provided for in the following chapters, where development of specific strategy components focuses attention on the detailed characteristics of selected industries.

A third problem arises from the averaging characteristics of industry data. Stacked against objectives these disclose whether the desired economic and technological potential exists within the industry as a whole. It does not answer this question from the viewpoint of an individual participant in the industry. This answer is often different for two reasons. First, the prospects for an individual firm in an industry can differ significantly from those of the industry as a whole. For example, the overall growth prospects in a mature industry, such as the detergents industry, can be satisfactory, whereas some firms in the industry face increasing price competition and a struggle for market shares. This condition occurs characteristically when the total industry capacity substantially exceeds the demand. Second, a firm considering an entry into an industry must take account of the cost of both entry and exit. It is frequently the case, for example, that certain industries (electronics in the early fifties, material handling in the mid-fifties, drugs in the late fifties) are generally recognized by the investing public as 'growth' areas. As a result, the earnings of firms in the areas become discounted over a long term and the price/earnings ratios tend to rise out of proportion to their real values. A firm contemplating diversifying into such an industry may be required to pay a greatly increased price for entry.

The cost of entry and exit is also significant for a different reason. If the market shares in the industry are widely distributed and the minimum investment required to enter is small, great mobility of firms in and out is to be expected. A member of the industry lacks security of his position, because an entrepreneur with a small capital and a 'garage loft' operation has easy access to the market. This condition is undesirable from the viewpoint of large established companies which lack the flexibility and quick response possessed by small firms. Contrariwise, small firms will find such an environment attractive.

To study these competitive considerations we shall first add several criteria which measure the competitive pressures and prospects in the industry to the list of economic criteria generated by objectives. Then we shall introduce another list of criteria labelled cost of entry criteria. These will assess individual industries for the relative cost of entry and for availability of attractive entries.

A fourth problem arises from the fact that a majority of diversifying firms expect to integrate the new activity into the parent operation. This adds *synergy criteria* to the economic and competitive criteria. These seek to further refine the assessment of an industry by measuring the potential joint economies and joint enhancements of performance which will result from the matching of competences possessed by the firm with those required by the new environment.

The preceding remarks set the stage for the decision flow diagram in external appraisal (Figure 8.3). The appraisal is triggered either by a need (existence of a diversification gap), or a management decision to find out whether there are outside opportunities which are more attractive than internal ones.

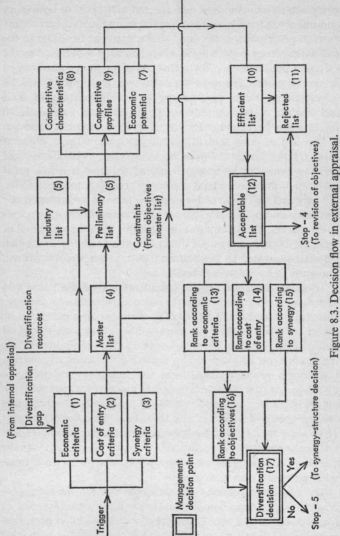

Figure 8.3. Decision flow in external appraisal.

The analysis commences with preparation of the three lists of criteria described above: *economic* (1), *cost of entry* (2), and *synergy* (3) denoted by the respective boxes in Figure 8.3. Expanded sample lists are presented in Tables 8.2, 8.3, and 8.4. As in previous samples of this kind, we have intentionally made the lists comprehensive ones. In actual practice, however, the list for a particular firm may be much shorter. For example, the firm which seeks a cash-rich acquisition for the first step in the programme would reduce its list of economic criteria virtually to the single item 'internal flexibility – cash reserves'. Most firms would end up with a longer list, depending on the nature of objectives sought through diversification. Together the three lists of criteria constitute the *master list* (4).

The second step in the analysis is to develop lists of candidate industries. This is done by first compiling a comprehensive industry list (5)* and then removing obvious misfits from it to obtain *preliminary industry list* (6). This is accomplished through use of the master list and the diversification resource limitations. Thus, for example, unless the firm is prepared to invest £175 million, the automobile industry will be quickly eliminated; digital computers also, unless the firm can make a £35 million investment. Some of the slow-growth industries, such as textiles or leather, may be eliminated, if one of the high-priority objectives is enhanced growth.

Data are now collected for each industry along the dimensions indicated by the criteria. For convenience these are grouped into three categories: *economic potential* (7), *competitive characteristics* (8), and *competitive profiles* (9). The procedure for constructing competitive profiles was developed in Chapter 5. This is a time-consuming phase of the analysis, but the data for it are generally available in government publications, trade literature, business periodicals, association publications, Moody's, and Standard and Poor's.

Next, the master list of criteria is applied to the above sets of industry characteristics to produce relative ratings of the industries. In the process some industries will be disqualified by threshold-goal criteria; some will pass, but will be demonstrably

* A useful starting point is Ref. 98.

TABLE 8.2 *Sample List of Economic Criteria for External Appraisal*

Priority	Objective	Criterion	Yardstick	Example: Firm's threshold-goals
	Proximate	ROI	ROI data: ● Historical ● Current ● Trend ● Variability	1. 10–20% return on equity 2. 20–30 times price/earnings
	Long-term	Growth	Trend in sales Trend in return on sales R&D as % of sales Technology prospects Life cycle position	1. 8–10% per annum sales growth 2. 5–10% per annum increase in earnings
		Stability	Dependence on single customer Seasonal stability Stability over business cycle	1. ±15% of sales over business cycle 2. ±20% of sales over season
	Contributes to proximate and long-term objectives	Competitive pressures	Status and trends in: ● Demand/capacity ● Control of market shares ● Price stability ● Earnings stability ● Mobility of competition	
	Flexibility	External	Diversity of technology* Diversity of demand*	1. Less than 30% of sales from single technology 2. 50/50 defence and industry sales
		Internal	Liquidity Cash reserves	1. Current ratio 4 : 1 2. Cash and securities ratio to current liabilities 1 : 1

* Note that these ratings are *relative* to the diversifying firm.

inferior on all counts to some other industry. Both of these sets are placed on the *rejected list* (11), the rest on the *efficient list* (10). An important characteristic of this list is that no industry is demonstrably superior to all others; while one industry may be outstanding on one criterion, there are others which are outstanding on different criteria.

While all industries on the efficient list are promising from the

TABLE 8.3 *Sample List of Cost of Entry Criteria*

Criterion	Yardstick	Example: Firm's constraints
Cost of entry	Price/earnings: • History • Current • Trends Price/book Critical size of entry Typical project payback period	1. No dilution of earnings/share 2. Maximum five-year payback
Availability of entries	Number and size distribution of firms Willing merger candidates Room for product-market new entries (demand/capacities)	

viewpoint of the objectives, not all of them will be acceptable, because of either internal or external constraints. It will be recalled that a list of such constraints is a part of the master list of objectives which was developed in Chapter 4. These are now applied to the list in order to weed out unacceptable industries.

Internal constraints are policy limitations self-imposed by the firm. Thus, as shown in Table 8.3, the firm's management may decide that diversification must not dilute the earnings/share of the present stockholders. This will exclude industries in which prevalent price/earnings ratios are substantially higher than the P/E ratio of the firm. Another constraint may be to avoid acquisitions in industries which have unions hostile to the unions of the firm. In this manner the firm seeks to avoid becoming a pawn in a jurisdictional struggle. A third constraint may be to avoid acquisitions in areas in which salary and wage scales are sharply out of line with those of the firm.

An important external constraint in diversification is the possibility of violation of the provisions of the American Sherman and Clayton Antitrust Acts. While this is usually not a problem for small firms, medium-sized and large firms which already have

TABLE 8.4 *Sample List of Synergy Criteria*

Criterion	Yardstick
Start-up synergy	Skills critical to success Common management skills Common organizational capacities Common equipment and factory Timing advantages
Operating synergy	Potential for new joint product-market Sharing of facilities Sharing of overhead Economics of scale in direct costs Sharing of R & D Sharing of general management

a substantial share of their markets are in danger that the very synergistic effects which the firm may seek will be interpreted by government agency to result in constraint of trade. Since the Clayton Act is vaguely worded, the problem of determining a potential violation is a technical one and should be handled by the corporation counsel rather than line management. This advice usually cannot be obtained in categorical form; the best to be hoped for is a judgement of the probability of adverse interpretation. Therefore, the position taken with respect to the acceptable list is again a matter of management risk attitude. Some may wish to eliminate all possibility of adverse rulings, while others may eliminate only the obvious violations and test others in action.*

Although the antitrust legislation is the most widely recognized external constraint, the firm may be further limited by others. Thus, for example, in certain states merger activity by banks is

* For further discussion of the antitrust problem see Ref. 99.

TABLE 8.5* Sample Evaluations of Selected Industries

Criteria	Air con-ditioning	Electronic controls	Metallurgy	Plastics fabrication
1. Expected economic environment				
a. Sales growth	9	10	9	7
b. Profit growth	5	7	6	5
c. Price stability	5	7	7	6
d. Excess productive capacity	5	8	6	4
e. Ease of entry by new firms into industry	6	8	7	4
SUBTOTAL	30	40	35	26
2. Stability of sales				
a. Stability of sales over business cycle	4	5	4	7
b. Dependence on single customer	9	7	7	7
SUBTOTAL	13	12	11	14
3. Breadth of combined product-market base				
a. Entry into fertile technological areas	2	8	7	6
b. Achievement of substantially broadened marketing competence	5	8	6	6
SUBTOTAL	7	16	13	12

TABLE 8.5

Operational compatibility				
a. Use of related technology	3	8	4	4
b. Use of related marketing skills	3	6	6	4
SUBTOTAL	6	14	10	8
5. Potential contribution of diversifying firms to acquired firm				
a. Technological contribution by diversifying firm to acquired firm	4	7	5	5
b. Potential usefulness of diversifying firm's marketing competence to the acquired firm	2	4	2	2
SUBTOTAL	6	11	7	7
6. Potential for joint product development	7	9	6	6
7. Availability of good prospects	5	5	5	6
GRAND TOTAL	74	107	87	79

* From Theodore A. Andersen, H. Igor Ansoff, Frank Norton, and J. Fred Weston, 'Planning for Diversification through Merger', *California Management Review*, vol. 1, no. 4, Summer, 1959.

severely circumscribed by law. Another example is a government policy requiring that prime contractors for weapons systems sub-contract a certain minimum percentage of the sterling value to outside subcontractors. As a result major systems contractors may prefer to avoid potential conflict of interests and refrain from acquiring manufacturers of sub-systems and components.

After the constraints have been used to reduce the efficient list the remainder is the *acceptable list* (12) of industries. It is possible that analysis will be terminated at this point if the acceptable list is empty (no industry survives from the efficient list) or if it contains very few suitable potential entries. To use the earlier example, if the automobile and computer industries were originally on the preliminary list, and were the only ones remaining on the acceptable list, the lack of available companies to acquire may discourage further interest.

If a decision to stop is made at this point, another revision of objectives will be needed by returning to (7) in the internal appraisal.

When the acceptable list is not empty, the next step is to rank entries in each list. Since each entry has a large number of different measurements, the problem is to reduce these to manageable proportions. One scheme which was used in an actual study is illustrated in Table 8.5.* The list of criteria is seen to be quite similar to ours, although differently grouped. A relative numerical rating was assigned to each yardstick on the scale of 1 to 10. The relative priority of the major criteria is indicated by the number of different yardsticks under it. Thus economic environment is given a maximum possible total of 50 compared with 10 for operational compatibility.†

Our suggestion is that rankings be constructed and consolidated in several steps. First, the multitude of economic yardsticks should be reduced to a threefold *rank according to economic*

* The table shows rankings of only four of some seventy industries studied.

† Table 8.5 shows that in the referenced study grand totals were added up. While this helped to narrow the efficient list somewhat, the results were found to be very sensitive to the relative priorities assigned to the respective criteria. The grand totals were used for reference only, and final selections were made on a judgement basis.

criteria (13), with one column each for the proximate, long-term, and flexibility objectives. The competitive pressures yardsticks are consolidated into the first two columns. Second, a list is produced which ranks industries according to *cost of entry* (14). In this list cost of entry and availability of entry yardsticks (Table 8.3) are consolidated into a single figure of merit; thus, this list will contain only one column.

Next, these two lists are consolidated into a three-column *rank according to objectives* (16) with the cost of entry being used to adjust the economic criteria ranks. A two-column *rank according to synergy criteria* (15) is next constructed. A start-up synergy column measures the effect on near-term profitability of new entries, and the operating synergy column on the long-term profitability. However, we delay a consolidation of this list with the rank of objectives, because full realization of synergy potential depends on the administrative strategy. This will be discussed in the next section.

We are finally in a position where a definitive *diversification decision* (17) can be made. The expansion opportunities analysed in the internal appraisal can now be compared with the lists produced in the external appraisal. A choice must be made to pursue expansion, diversification, or both. The factors which force the choice one way or another have been discussed in Chapter 7. The following variants of the decision to diversify are possible.

1. In rare cases, when internal appraisal forecasts a decline in the firm's present business in spite of all possible measures taken to reverse it, the indicated decision is to liquidate the firm as it now exists and to reinvest the proceeds into diversification, thus creating a new type of firm.

2. When the expansion forecast shows level sales or slow growth, a somewhat less drastic decision is to keep the present business, but to devote most of available resources to diversification. This appears to have been the path taken by Textron and W. R. Grace Company.

3. When both expansion and diversification opportunities are only moderately promising, but, upon comparison, no diversification opportunity is sufficiently superior to justify the added risks and the loss in synergy, the previous commitment of resources to

142

expansion would be maintained. Diversification would be limited to the use of the residual resources.

4. When diversification opportunities are attractive enough to sacrifice expansion moves and even relinquish some parts of present business, the revised forecast (7), the expansion (11), and the expansion resources (12) on Figure 8.2 are adjusted downward and the diversification gap (10) and resources for diversification (13) are correspondingly increased. Before analysis can proceed, a check should be made to see whether the external appraisal needs to be modified.

5. When the information obtained through the external appraisal is judged to be inadequate to commit the firm either way, several courses may be pursued:

a. A decision to develop more information may be made. If so, appropriate parts of the external appraisal (particularly parts 5 to 9) are put on a continuing basis until enough information is developed.

b. Another, not infrequent, decision is that information about diversification is inherently less reliable than information about expansion and that the advantages of diversification are not worth the risk. The firm will pursue the expansion strategy.

c. A third is a decision by default. An attempt to formulate strategy will lead nowhere, but the firm ought to 'look around' for individual attractive opportunities. This case of companies in search for opportunities, without a clear idea of what they are looking for or a clear management commitment to act, is descriptive of a number of so-called 'diversification programmes' in American firms.

The particular course of action chosen and its timing will again depend on the risk philosophy of the firm's management. Thus, for example, managements with aversion to high risks would probably avoid facing decision 1. – liquidation of present business – until the last moment in the hope that 'things will straighten out'. They would also be disinclined to follow decision 4. – curtailment of expansion and possible divestment from some products in favour of diversification. Courses 3. – diversify using excess resources – and 2. – keep present business, invest only in diversification – would be prepared in that order.

Any of the decisions except 5. moves the analysis to the next stage.

SYNERGY AND STRUCTURE*

The external appraisal produced two lists which rank industries on objectives and synergy.

The synergy rankings can be viewed as modifiers of the objectives ratings; to the economic and competitive assessment of industries they add an assessment of joint performance advantages which the firm may enjoy in each industry. However, it is essential to recall that these are only potential advantages, estimated from a superposition of profiles and that they will not be realized unless the diversifying firm provides the appropriate organizational environment. To illustrate this point, suppose that a manufacturer of medium-sized electric motors in the South of England acquires a Scottish firm which makes fractional-horsepower motors. Strong potential synergy is evident in engineering, purchasing, manufacturing, and perhaps even marketing. However, distance and management interfere, and the two divisions are made to operate completely independently of each other. Actual synergy will be negligible.

Thus synergy and structure of the firm's organization are seen to be dependent on each other. The relation can be resolved by making structure follow synergy. In this case the post-diversification organization is adjusted so as to maximize synergy. When strong synergy happens to exist at all levels of the firm, a tightly integrated organization would be used. Top management would be made responsible not only for strategic but also for key operating decisions, such as pricing, production, and respective inventory levels. The acquisition would be absorbed into the respective functional departments of the firm and profit and loss

---

* This section is based on a paper by H. I. Ansoff and J. F. Weston titled 'Merger Objectives and Organizational Structure'.[100] Our concern here is solely with the effect of organization on strategy formulation. Two other organizational questions are how should the firm organize *in order* to diversify and how should it handle the post-acquisition transition in order to assure effective integration of the new subsidiary. These questions are examined in Ref. 101.

responsibility would be centralized.* When synergy is strong only in general management, but not in functional areas, a decentralized organization is indicated. The acquisition would be set up as a division and assigned profit and loss responsibility. Finally, when synergy potential is weak up and down the organization, a holding company structure is indicated. This would occur, for example, when the diversified firm finds itself in shipping, electronics and chemicals at the same time. To avoid negative synergy top management will delegate the strategic as well as operating decisions, reserving for itself only the area of corporate finance.

If structure is to follow synergy, the acquiring management should have both the desire and the flexibility to change with the occasion. Quite frequently this will not be the case. Top managers who were brought up in internally oriented skills, such as engineering or manufacturing, often feel uncomfortable in the loosely structured environment of a holding company; but managers from marketing, and particularly finance, frequently prefer it. Furthermore, the respective groups perform better in a familiar environment.

Aside from management preferences, firms do not usually have the flexibility of structure to follow the vagaries of synergy. Nor would the synergistic advantages always offset the resulting costs and inefficiencies of structural change. This would be true, for example, when the acquisition is relatively small but very different from the parent. Rather than revise the overall organizational concept, the firm will usually force the acquisition to fit into the already existing structure and not worry about synergistic effects.†

Whether synergy shall follow structure or vice versa is a major top management decision. This decision needs to be made at this point, rather than delayed until an actual acquisition is in hand,

---

* These generalizations are a function of the size of the firm and apply to small and medium-sized firms. In large firms, which already have a decentralized profit and loss responsibility, our comments would be applicable at the level of a division.

† This is sometimes called 'loving your acquisition to death' – rather than being left alone it frequently is enveloped by well-meaning, voluminous, and poorly informed advice from the corporate headquarters.

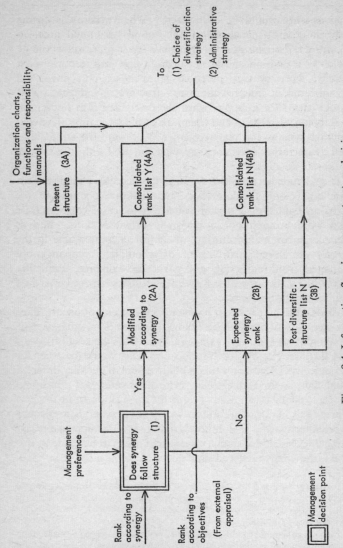

Figure 8.4. Information flow in synergy-structure decision.

because it affects strategy and hence the search and evaluation of opportunities. Its effect on strategy formulation is illustrated in Figure 8.4. The first step is management's answer to *does synergy follow structure* (1). If the answer is yes, a new *modified rank according to synergy* (2A) is produced by modifying the rankings on synergy produced in external appraisal to take account of organizational mismatches. Generally, the respective levels of expected synergy will be lower than before, and relative order of ranking will undergo some change.

If the decision is to change the organization so as to maximize synergy the *expected synergy list* (2B) will be the same as the list in the external appraisal. However, to each industry an appropriate *post-diversification organizational structure* (3B) is assigned. For example, a firm in railway signals and brakes which diversifies into military electronics should give the new subsidiary a near complete freedom of action. The same firm acquiring a company in diesel locomotives should use either a functional or a closely integrated divisional structure.

In either case (2A) or (2B) the next step can now be taken of consolidating the synergy ranking with the ranking according to objectives. In each case a final *consolidated rank* (4A) or (4B) is produced for the industries on the acceptable list.

CHAPTER 9

Choice of Strategy

The end products of managers' work are decisions and actions.
PETER DRUCKER

THE PROBLEM

THE synergy-structure decision moves strategy formulation into its final stage. The first step is to construct alternative portfolios of product-market entries which are individually large enough to be competitive, which are related to each other, and which can be undertaken within the resources of the firm. The first section of this chapter is concerned with a procedure for constructing such alternative portfolios.

In the process of selecting the diversification product-market scope, two problems, which have remained in the background until now, come into focus. The first is how to trade off competing demands of proximate, long-term, and flexibility objectives. Put somewhat more generally, the problem is how to select the preferred product-market scope from alternatives, each of which is measured by several incommensurate yardsticks. Although extensive literature exists on this subject, management science can offer only partial assistance to the decision maker. Some specific procedures are described in the second section.

The second problem, which so far has been only partially explored in this book, is how to allow for the risk associated with strategic decisions. Several sources of risk and uncertainty are discussed in the third section. This is followed by a brief review of decision rules which are commonly discussed in management science. A somewhat complex procedure is suggested by which several of these rules can be brought to bear on selection of the product-market scope and the growth vector.

The remaining two components of strategy – competitive advantage and synergy – follow selection of scope and help sharpen the firm's search and evaluation of opportunities. Procedures for selecting each are discussed in the fourth and the fifth sections, respectively.

The final section of the chapter summarizes the adaptive search theory of strategic decisions and discusses the manner in which requirements set forth in Chapter 2 have been met.

PRODUCT-MARKET PORTFOLIOS

The synergy-structure decision results in a consolidated list of industries ranked on each of the major objectives. This list is the basis for selection of the diversification product-market scope. Except in unusual circumstances, no single industry will be preferable to all others for all of the firm's objectives. If the unusual does occur, the choice is clear and the analysis can proceed to selection of other components of strategy. More usually, industries which are preferable for proximate profitability will be inferior to others on long-term objectives. Industries which would contribute most to flexibility will generally be deficient on near-term profitability because of lower synergy with the firm.

To provide the firm with an attractive overall product-market posture it is necessary therefore to consider alternative *portfolios* of industries. One approach to alternatives is to construct all possible combinations of industries from the consolidated rank list and to measure them against objectives and other relevant constraints. This procedure is feasible if the choice strategy can be programmed on a computer. If analysis by hand is to be used, the number of such alternatives may become unmanageable (in one study the consolidated list contained some forty different industries). Under these conditions a judgemental trial-and-error method can be used to better advantage to select a handful of the most promising portfolios.

The flexibility objective is attained through a diversity of different entries; it requires, therefore, a large number of entries in the portfolio. The other two major objectives exert an influence toward a small number of entries. The reasons are:

1. A large number of different entries entails an accumulation of entry costs which will depress profitability. The cost of an

entry is relatively independent of its size, since the same minimum learning costs have to be incurred for a £500,000 as for a £10 million entry. This applies to all types of firms, but the restriction is less stringent for non-integrated ones. However, even an investment trust faces a fixed commission cost per transaction. A very widely diversified investment portfolio can generate a substantial entry cost.

2. Once acquired, many distinct and different entries will cost more to operate because of a lack of synergy and dilution of management attention. For a given entry a minimum management commitment is required, regardless of its size. Thus even in an investment trust the investment officer must 'manage' each entry through keeping track of its performance and prospects. Clearly the load on an operating manager is much greater.

3. For many types of entry there is a minimum *critical mass* below which the chances of success drop off quickly. This applies primarily to firms which acquire or create whole operating units, such as divisions or companies. It does not apply to firms which acquire a part of the equity in an operating unit. Although this practice is confined largely to investment firms, some operating firms acquire a part interest in another firm and many go into joint ventures.*

Critical mass is the market share which a firm must obtain in order to become fully competitive on price and cost. Its attainment calls for an ability to assimilate the start-up costs and then to build a direct cost base large enough to absorb competitively the indirect costs of the business. Further, the firm must be able to attain the critical mass within a reasonable span of time, comparable to the normal product development lead time for the industry. Failure to do so creates strong pressures to abandon the venture. In small firms, failure to build up quickly to the critical mass may lead to bankruptcy.

Failure to make realistic estimates of the critical mass has been dramatically illustrated in the digital computer industry. A number of firms sought to enter the industry apparently without having anticipated the very high start-up cost and the very large

* In the last two examples there may be another type of 'critical mass' – a requirement to acquire a controlling interest.

development, marketing, and service costs. Three medium-sized firms found themselves stretched beyond their means and quit; three very large firms hung on, but showed every evidence of surprise and disappointment at the amount of red ink they were forced to incur.

While critical mass is the minimum size of entry needed in order to be competitive, entries which are larger than critical mass are to the firm's advantage, because of large volume and consequent stronger competitive position.

Since the overall size of the portfolio is limited by the total resources available for diversification (see internal appraisal, Chapter 8), the most attractive portfolios will be the result of a compromise between sizes of individual entries and their total number, subject to the critical mass constraint.

A procedure for developing portfolios of product-market alternatives is illustrated in Figure 9.1. Several provisional *product-market scope alternatives* or portfolios (1) are selected by judgement (or the entire list of possibilities enumerated for computer processing). At this point an alternative scope may be as narrow as an industry or part of an industry (if the firm has been fortunate enough to find one which has good potential for all objectives); or, it may be a combination of two or three industries selected and matched on their respective contribution to objectives.

Next, each entry in the portfolio is assigned a *critical mass* and a tentative *size of entry* (2). The assignments are based on competitive profiles data previously developed in the external appraisal. The total resource requirement generated by a product-market portfolio is next tested for *feasibility* (3) by comparing it with the resources available, as determined in the internal appraisal. If the scope is not feasible, it is reduced and again tested for critical mass.

Alternatives which pass the feasibility test are next classified for their growth vector properties by constructing a matrix similar to Figure 7.3. This serves three purposes:

1. Within an industry a sub-division into several related product-mission combinations helps sharpen the choice of product-market scope. Thus, a firm which originally had

151

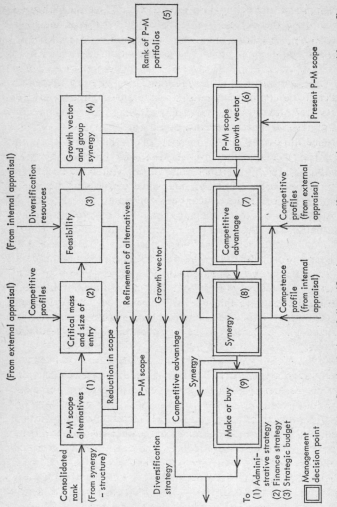

Figure 9.1. Decision flow in choice of diversification strategy (for expansion strategy, start with step 5).

electronics as a diversification alternative, may split this into several distinct alternatives, such as military and space systems, conventional components, exotic components, materials, and consumer products.

2. Within a portfolio, the growth vector matrix relates different industries to each other with respect to their economic and technological foundations. This makes it possible to rank portfolios on the economic and cost of entry objectives.

3. The common thread delineated by the matrix permits synergy estimates for each portfolio.

The set of portfolios defined and measured against objectives with the assistance of the growth vector is next ranked (5) on each major objective. The result is a list similar to the consolidated list, but containing portfolios for its entries, rather than for industries.

WEIGHTING OF ALTERNATIVES

The stage is set for a major decision point at which the firm commits itself to a particular product-market scope and growth vector. At first glance this would appear to be quite simple; the portfolio which offers the best performance for the firm's objectives is the one to choose. In practice this turns out to be a difficult process. Each portfolio is measured by three ratings, one each in proximate, long-term, and flexibility objectives. These are in the nature of apples, pears, and oranges. Each contributes to a different aspect of the firm's performance; each is measured by a different yardstick; and an increase in one usually involves a decrease in the others. There is no obvious way in which they can be combined to produce a single figure of merit for each scope.

This dilemma of reconciling non-commensurate and non-colinear objectives is not an issue in the behavioral theory of the firm. There it is asserted that real-life firms do not deal with multiple alternatives, but rather search for one alternative at a time. When an alternative is found which satisfies the firm's aspirations on *all* of the dimensions of the objective, the search stops and the alternative is adopted.[102] Thus, no combined figure of merit is needed.

While there is evidence (cited by Cyert and March) that some conservative firms do behave this way, there is also evidence that more progressive firms do not. Further, since our interest is in improving and not just in describing decision processes, it is our strong recommendation that firms should by all means take advantage of opportunities to select from multiple alternatives, even though the selection process may be complex and imprecise. The recommendation is based on a common experience, that in the absence of some absolute standard (and business firms have few of these!), the value of a course of action can be more clearly perceived if it is viewed against the background of alternatives.

This, however, leaves us with the problem outlined above. One helpful feature of our method of strategy formulation is the multi-stage process of narrowing of the field of alternatives, which reduces the final list of portfolio scopes to a relatively small number, sometimes to a single acceptable alternative. Another useful feature is the assignment of priorities to the respective objectives, since these can be used as 'weights' to compute an overall weighted rank for each of the remaining alternatives in a manner similar to the one illustrated in Table 8.5. It must be recognized, however, that different numerical weights may lead to different choices. Several weighting schemes should be tried, therefore, and further subjected to consistency tests, such as the Churchman-Ackoff Test.[103]

The result of these evaluations may be a dominant choice which is not sensitive to reasonable weighting schemes. More frequently, several alternative 'best' choices will emerge depending on the weights. Mathematical manipulation stops here and the full range of results and assumptions should be presented to the responsible executive for his final decision. Thus, while management science can offer help in clarifying choices, the final decision and the responsibility for it remain with the executive.

ALLOWING FOR RISK AND UNCERTAINTY

The weighting procedures described above do not resolve a problem which has a major influence on final choice. This is the problem of risk.*

* In the following we shall use the word risk in a non-technical sense to

Risk enters the problem in two ways. First, we had to recognize at the outset that our ability to foresee the future in any detail is limited to only certain foreseeable events and that we have every reason to expect that other events, unforeseeable at present, have a high likelihood of occurring. We sought to provide for unforeseeable events through the goals-threshold method for setting objectives and also through the flexibility objective.

However, the foreseeable events also contain several elements of risk. First, assuming that our projections of future business conditions are accurate, the expectations of the firm's success in any given industry are at best probability judgements. The probable may not materialize, and the firm may perform very differently from expectations. It may do much better than expected, or it may fail altogether. Second, the projections of business conditions on which these expectations are based are themselves estimates of probable events. Third, the activities contemplated by the firm will impinge on those of other firms which may react through competition and try to minimize the effectiveness of our actions.

Thus the expectations from respective diversification prospects depend on three sources of uncertainty: uncertainties in estimation of results, uncertainties in projecting the environment, and uncertainties in competitive reaction. To a limited extent we have sought to provide for the third in the external appraisal through analysis of competitive conditions and of the cost of entry. If the contemplated entry is into an industry in which market shares are widely distributed and no major competitor dominates the industry, the provisions made in external appraisal are probably adequate. However, if the entry will have a major impact on the industry and if it is to be made against major competitors, an analysis of competitive consequences needs to be made.

As discussed earlier (see Chapter 6), there is a body of mathematics called *game theory* concerned with problems of competi-

---

denote the impact of imperfect information on decision making. As discussed earlier, in mathematical literature risk is a condition under which either the occurrence or the outcome of alternatives is not certain but is assigned probabilities.

tive conflict.* As a tool for solution of business problems, game theory has achieved limited success. The fault is in part with the mathematical part of the theory which is still capable of solving only very elementary games and in part with management theory, since it has failed so far to construct more than a few 'games' of practical value. While still far from being a practical management tool, game theory offers an extremely powerful and useful concept for analysis of strategic problems in which interaction among competitors has a strong influence on choice of strategy. Therefore, if any of the product-market scope alternatives do pose major competitive implications, they should be examined from the view point of game theory, if only to define and recognize the counter-strategies which the competition may employ.† As a result of such study, the respective ratings and hence the ranks of the product-market alternatives should be adjusted.

RULES FOR DECISION

During the Appraisals the uncertainties of estimation and of prediction have been handled without an explicit recognition of probable errors in the estimates. A 'most likely' environment was constructed and the 'most likely' performance ascribed to the firm. This was necessary to avoid overcomplicating an already complex analysis. However, at the short strokes of strategy selection, consideration of risk must be introduced more explicitly.

There is another considerable body of mathematical literature, generally referred to as *decision theory*, which is concerned with decision making under imperfect information.[105] It is based on a variety of what W. T. Morris[106] calls 'principles of choice' – decision rationales imputed to the decision maker. Unfortunately, there is at present very little understanding of the extent to which these rationales correspond to the ways in which a business decision maker actually does make decisions. A major point of contention among the various theories is the manner in which the

* An excellent introduction to the theory is found in Ref. 104.

† In doing this the firm will need help from a competent management scientist.

executive compares the risk-gain properties of one alternative with those of another.

Nevertheless, decision theory is useful as a 'truth and consequence' device. By tracing the consequences of different risk-gain assumptions the decision maker can see what the resulting strategy would be under different principles of choice.* To provide such perspective we shall briefly describe several of the most common decisions rules found in the literature.[107]

The alternative approaches are shown in Table 9.1. The aspiration level decision rule, briefly referred to earlier, merely sets a minimum performance level required of an alternative. Alternatives which are below the level are rejected, those which equal or exceed it are accepted. The rule works when one alternative is being examined at a time. When several alternatives are being considered, the method has no way of discriminating among them.

The goals-threshold method, which we have introduced and discussed in detail in this book, is a step beyond the aspiration level. It rejects undesirable opportunities below the threshold, permits us to assess relative desirability of a *single* opportunity by its place within the threshold-goal range, and permits comparison of several alternatives.

Both of the preceding rules measure the returns and say nothing about the probability of occurrence. The most probable choice method, shown third, neglects the returns and deals with probabilities alone. It has merit when the probability of some particular environmental condition is much greater than that of all others. For example, if good business conditions are overwhelmingly indicated, the manager may wish to take a chance on selecting a strategy which does not make provisions for a depression. A problem arises, however, when some low-probability event neglected in the strategy has the potential of causing a complete disaster for the firm. Thus, by placing all of its bets on boom conditions, the firm may lose liquidity to a point, where, say, a mere 20 per cent drop in sales could lead to bankruptcy. Thus, no provision for risk is made.

* The actual application of the model is not something the manager himself usually would do. Most would require the help of a trained management scientist.

TABLE 9.1 *Principles of Choice*

Approach	Procedure	Selection
1. Aspiration level	Set minimum values to be attained on each objective.	Select strategy which reaches or exceeds aspiration level for all objectives.
2. Goals-threshold	Set minimum values to be attained and also goal values desired.	Reject all strategies below threshold. Select strategy which gives best weighted rating.
3. Most probable choice	Assign probabilities to respective objectives ratings.	Select strategy which has the greatest probability.
4. Expected value	For each strategy multiply objective value by probability of success and add.	Select strategy with the greatest sum.
5. Rating/probability exchange	Through judgement determine the value to firm of each rating/probability combination. Add values for each strategy.	Select strategy with greatest sum.

The expected value approach, (4) in the table, assumes that all decision makers balance risk versus gain in the same way and that they compare alternatives by the product of the returns and the probability of its occurrence.

Finally, the rating-probability exchange method differs from the expected value method in that the choice of an equivalent risk-returns combination is left to the decision maker and is not assumed to be measured by the product of the two.

The expected value and the rating-probability exchange method both suffer from the deficiency that no course of action is rejected outright because it may contain a particularly unfavourable outcome. However, in selecting its strategy the firm will probably want to reject alternatives which have a substantial probability of losing money, even though their expected value may be attractive. This kind of provision for risk can be made by application of simulation techniques.[108] This is a much more difficult process than application of the preceding decision rules, because it requires that a *probability distribution* of outcomes be obtained for *each* alternative.

It is seen from the preceding that the weighting, the game theory, and the decision rules are addressed to complementary aspects of the problem. The first deals with a combination of incommensurate yardsticks, the second with actions by competition, and the third with the uncertainties in the action outcomes and in behaviour of the environment.

For the purpose of strategy selection, we recommend an approach which is a combination of weighting, game theory, goals-threshold rule, and expected value, or the rating-probability exchange rule. It would proceed as follows.

1. The threshold minimums are applied to reject alternatives which do not meet the minimums established for each objective. This has a secondary effect of eliminating undesirable risks.

2. Wherever appropriate, the rating and hence relative rank of alternatives is reviewed and adjusted through the use of a game matrix which contains possible counter-strategies of competition.

3. Probability is assigned to each alternative for each objective. This is a combination probability which accounts for uncertainties of both estimation and forecasting. It is also a simple-minded

probability: its value p_s denotes chances of success of the alternative, its complement $(1-p_s)$ the probability of failure. The rank of an alternative for each objective is weighted in accordance to the weight of priority assigned to the objective. The 'value' of each alternative is computed using either expected value or judgement on the probability-returns exchange for each alternative-objective combination. The alternative with the highest 'value' is selected.

The following presents a simple example.

TABLE 9.2

Objective Product–market scope	Proximate (2)	Long–term (1)	Flexibility (3)	
$(P-M)_1$	(1,0.7)	(3,0.9)	(1,0.4)	Priorities (3 is highest)
$(P-M)_2$	(2,0.6)	(1,0.8)	(3,0.2)	
$(P-M)_3$	(3,0.8)	(2,0.5)	(2,0.9)	Probability Rank (3 is highest)

The computation of the expected value would look as follows:

$(P-M)_1$: $(2 \times 1 \times 0.7) + (1 \times 3 \times 0.9) + (3 \times 1 \times 0.4) = 5.3$
$(P-M)_2$: $(2 \times 2 \times 0.6) + (1 \times 1 \times 0.8) + (3 \times 3 \times 0.2) = 5.0$
$(P-M)_3$: $(2 \times 3 \times 0.8) + (1 \times 2 \times 0.5) + (3 \times 2 \times 0.9) = 11.2$

$(P-M)_3$ is clearly superior to the other two product-market scopes. Other priorities would be tried in a similar manner. In this case it is significant that the choice remains the same even when the objectives are assigned the same priorities.

The evaluation scheme proposed above is one of many similar ones which can be constructed. No particular merit can be claimed for it, other than the inclusion in one evaluation of all the major factors which affect the decision. In actual strategy selection, it will be useful to evaluate the alternatives in several different ways and to present to the decision maker the sensitivities of outcomes to different assumptions.

COMPETITIVE ADVANTAGE

Beyond specifying the scope and the growth vector, it is to the firm's advantage to be on the lookout for individual opportunities within the scope which offer an unusual promise. There are two ways in which such opportunities can be identified: 1. in relation to characteristics of other products and markets and 2. through the general characteristics of the competitive environment.

Turning to the latter first, we have already identified some environmental characteristics which may make a new entry attractive to the firm. One of these is the cost of entry for a new competitor. A large firm backed by substantial resources would prefer the cost of entry and exit to be relatively high. Once having made the entry, the firm can feel secure from ingress by new 'fly by night' competition. A small firm, on the other hand, may prefer the advantages of low cost and flexible response.

Another characteristic which a firm may consciously seek is a favourable demand to capacity relationship. If the total capacity equals or exceeds demand, the competitive environment is due for a shakeout, even if the demand is growing. This occurred recently in the transistor industry and appears to be currently taking place in the digital computer industry. On the other hand, outward evidence of slow growth may conceal a very attractive demand to capacity prospect. An excellent example is provided by the case of the Sylvania Corporation in its success in fluorescent light starters. At the time a self-starting unit was introduced, light starters were a highly competitive item of low profitability. In the face of the apparent prospect of declining demand, several of the major suppliers decided to get out of the light starter business. Sylvania, on the other hand, saw in these actions a prospect of declining capacity which more than offset the decline in demand. It judged the demand to capacity ratio to be favourable, stayed in the business, and turned it into a profitable item.*

* This anecdote is based on a verbal communication from Don G. Mitchell, vice-chairman of General Telephone and Electronics Inc.

A third characteristic which a firm may require in its entries is competitive dominance. As mentioned earlier, this may be attained by means of patent protection, cost of entry, or a dominant share of the market. Two widely diversified companies known to the author have consciously sought industries which are *small enough* to permit the new entrants to acquire major positions.

An ability to distinguish advantageous product-market trends and opportunities is more subtle, but often more rewarding than perception of the competitive forces. Early perception by Sears of the move to suburban shopping enabled the company to outdistance Montgomery Ward. GM's perception in the 1920s of the trend to more luxurious personal transportation, coupled with the cleverly designed appeal of 'much more value for a little higher price', contributed to reversing the relative competitive positions of Ford and GM.[109] Litton's early perception of the advent of miniaturized airborne computers and a revival of need for inertial guidance enabled the firm to surge forward in military electronics.

While potentially rewarding, search for competitive advantage through anticipating trends is also potentially expensive. Ford's fiasco with the Edsel is a classic example of a mistimed anticipation. Less spectacular, but probably very costly, has been RCA's premature attempt to commercialize colour television.

The search for a competitive advantage can be helped by a classification of product-market opportunities. Thus competing products can be classified into one of three following categories:

1. A *breakthrough* product which offers either a radical performance advantage over competition, a drastically lower price, or, in a highly desirable but unlikely situation, it may offer both. Usually such products incorporate a technology which is novel to the particular customer need. The automobile was a breakthrough product in the 1890s, radio in the 1920s, television in the 1940s, transistors in the 1950s.

2. A *competitive* product is one which shows no clear-cut advantage over other products. It is competitive in the sense that it represents a particular compromise of cost and performance characteristics. Some of these are superior to competition, others are at a disadvantage. A typical example of competitive products

is the group of synthetic fibres available on today's markets: Dacron, nylon, Kodel, and Orlon.

3. An *improved* product which lies between the above two, while not radically different, can be shown to be clearly superior to others (usually better performance at competitive price, or lower price for same performance). It will usually be the result of incorporation of recent advances in the technology which had previously been applied to the particular market need.

The characteristics of the demand for products can be similarly classified.

1. *Established* demand exists when a particular customer need has been previously serviced by existing products.

2. Under *latent* demand a group of potential customers is identified. The customers are aware of their needs, but no product has so far been offered to fill them.

3. Under *incipient* demand there is no awareness of need on the part of prospective customers; however, a trend can be recognized which points toward emergence of future need.

The important difference between types of demand lies in the cost of gaining acceptance for a new product. Under existing demand acceptance is gained by proving superiority of the new product over others available. When this superiority appears self-evident, as with a breakthrough product, the cost is relatively low and competitive potential correspondingly high. Under latent demand the customers need to be sold not on a relative asset but on the idea of the product. They will want to have its performance capabilities demonstrated, they will want to be assured of its reliability, and they will want to be convinced that it really fills the need. Above all, they will need to be sold on the price.

Incipient demand requires the highest cost for customer acceptance. Two additional elements of cost must be considered. One is the cost of 'educating' the customer; the other, oddly enough, is the cost of finding the customers. This cost has to be incurred on the embarrassingly frequent occasions when the engineering department of a firm invents what has been aptly called 'a solution in search of a problem' – a product for which no specific group of customers has been identified. The confidence level in whatever estimates are arrived at for incipient demand is the lowest of the three cases. The uncertainty in the estimates of market size must now be compounded with the uncertainty of existence of the market in the first place.

Aside from costs, the three types of demand clearly imply very different timing for product introduction. The shortest delay is incurred under existing demand; the longest, in converting incipient to existing demand.

The grouping above of products and markets offers a means for examining the product-market scope for trends and directions which are competitively attractive and which also contribute to the objectives. From this examination the firm can select an additional strategy component which we have previously defined as the *competitive advantage*. Table 9.3 is helpful in this analysis.

The table offers a rough classification which matches product-market types to the objectives they can best meet. The breakthrough product is seen to contribute to the firm's flexibility. The timing of the contribution will depend on the type of demand to which the product is addressed. The improved and competitive products may contribute to either the proximate or the long-term objectives, or to both, depending on the nature of the demand.

TABLE 9.3 *Objectives and Competitive Advantage*

Demand / Product	Existing	Latent	Incipient
Breakthrough	flexibility		
Improved Competitive	Proximate	Proximate and long-term	Long-term

Generally speaking, in seeking breakthrough products the firm pursues the strongest possible competitive advantage. However, the estimate of the advantage must be tempered by the higher costs of opening latent and particularly incipient markets. Pursuit of these calls for a strategy of gradual resource commitment in order to take advantage of timing on the one hand and the natural evolution of markets on the other. In this manner the firm avoids the extra burden of being a single-handed trail blazer. In some ways, anticipation of latent markets with existing or improved products (as in the case of G M and Sears mentioned above) appears to be the most attractive of all, since it takes advantage of astute timing and may not require a major financial exposure. An attempt to open up incipient markets with improved or competitive products is the riskiest and potentially the most expensive course. A firm which follows it undertakes the thankless task of blazing a trail for other firms without any particular advantage over them.

To summarize, the competitive advantage adds a dimension to strategy, both in search and in evaluation of opportunities. Although some straightforward steps can be taken to select the competitive advantage, really successful results require uncommon skills in anticipating trends in markets and in technology. The ability to anticipate is greatly enhanced by a knowledge of the industry and its environment. This is one reason why concentric diversification to related areas offers better opportunities for a competitive advantage than is offered by conglomerate diversification.

SYNERGY COMPONENT OF STRATEGY

A natural companion to the competitive advantage is the synergy component of strategy. This requires that opportunities within the scope possess characteristics which will enhance synergy. The process for determining the synergy component was described in detail in Chapter 5. To recapitulate briefly, the firm's competence profile is superimposed on top of the competitive profile of the product-market scope (or some part of it). The areas of reinforcement show areas of potential synergy described in terms of individual skills, specialized facilities, organizational or management skills. The items with the strongest potential are selected for the synergy component of strategy.

In constructing and comparing the profiles it is important to avoid mistaking an abundant competence for an outstanding one. A classic example of such confusion was provided by the aircraft industry after World War II, when many of its members sought to diversify into a variety of products fabricated of aluminium. In retrospect this strategy appears to have been wrong in two ways. First, the specialized organizational structure of the aircraft industry, with attendant high overhead and labour costs, precluded it from being competitive in industrial and consumer aluminium fabrication. Secondly, the fabrication competence *was not* a critical success ingredient in most applications which were attempted. In consumer applications (skis, canoes) merchandising was the skill; in industrial applications (self-powered wheelbarrows) trouble-free continuous operation under poor maintenance and abuse was required. Interestingly enough, one venture which appears to have succeeded was a high-quality, high-margin item marketed under very special conditions (aluminium coffins).

Another possible confusion to be avoided is the use of the same terminology in different industries to describe activities which are not necessarily identical. For example, the term 'systems' is becoming popular for describing large-scale non-military industrial projects. Since the defence industry has a highly developed capability for managing military weapons systems, the claim is often made that this 'systems management skill' is applicable to the large industrial projects. While this may be true in some instances, the mere use of identical terms does not guarantee complete similarity. In fact, a more detailed examination of the respective management needs would probably disclose some important differences between the two types of systems management job.

The synergy component and competitive advantage need to be made compatible; ideally, one should be an extension of the other. Unless this is done, they may cancel each other. For example, the selected competitive advantage may call for opportunities which utilize a geographic shift in the demand pattern, while the synergy component may require that the opportunities fit into the current marketing and distribution facilities.

This feedback relationship is shown in Figure 9.1, to which we can now return after a long digression. The figure shows that choice of *product-market scope* and of *growth vector* (6), of *synergy* (7), and of *competitive advantage* component (8) of strategy complete the job of strategy formulation, except for the decision on the method of growth. This is discussed in the next section.

Before proceeding, however, it should be pointed out that strategy formulation for *expansion strategy* follows a similar pattern. Since the product-market scope is not changed, steps (1) to (4) deal with redefinition of the growth vector and allocation of resources among its components.

ACQUISITION VERSUS INTERNAL GROWTH – THE MAKE OR BUY DECISION

The process of strategy selection was carried out in broad terms without reference to whether the firm will grow by acquisition or develop from within. The decision on whether to 'make or buy' new product-markets is needed before strategy can be implemented.

Both acquisition and internal development assume many forms. The former varies from licensing, to purchase of developed products, to mergers with another firm; the latter, from addition of new products to major organizational changes to make room for new skills and competences.

Two primary variables influence the choice between the major alternatives. These are the start-up cost and the timing. In internal development the costs are incurred by product development and introduction, and by acquisition of new facilities and organizations. Acquisition pays for these costs too; however, over and above them is a premium which frequently has to be paid as a compensation for the risks which had been taken by the seller to develop the property and the competences being sold.

Because of this premium, it is sometimes argued that internal development is cheaper. This is not necessarily the case, because, in risky undertakings, budgeting for internal development has to include a risk allowance to provide for the variances in the estimates and the uncertainties of the results. There are cases, however, in which the premium paid on acquisition may not be an accurate reflection of the risks which have been taken. Thus, a firm which seeks to diversify into a currently glamorous growth industry is forced to pay a premium which may be excessive.

In some cases the choice between acquisition and internal development is forced in favour of the latter. This will occur when the current price/earnings ratio in the new industry is much higher than that of the firm itself. A desire to avoid large dilutions in earnings per share may make acquisition out of the question. The choice may also be forced by lack of attractive acquisition opportunities in the new industry. The choice may be forced the other way when the competitive structure in the new industry leaves no room for a significant new entry.

In internal development the timing of entry consists of two elements. 1. The normal product development cycle. This may vary from six months to four years depending on technological and marketing complexity of the product. 2. The time span required to acquire new skills and competence. This can vary from one to five or six years. The total time span will depend on the degree of synergy between the new product-market and the firm.

In acquisition of a firm the delay is theoretically only as long as the time to consummate the transaction. In practice a time delay is added during which the acquisition is introduced into the parent organization. However, even after this provision it generally takes much longer to develop than to acquire a firm. If a product, rather than a firm, is being acquired, the time span may vary from the time it takes to tool and market, when synergy is strong, to several years, when a complete range of supporting competences has to be developed.

The pros and cons of acquisition versus internal development can be related to the components of synergy, as shown in Table 9.4.

As the second entry in the table indicates, internal development is indicated when the start-up synergy is strong, even if operating synergy is weak. Although there may not be operating economies, the firm's competence pattern assures a fast start and low risk. Exceptions in favour of acquisition may occur 1. when the needs of the firm or instability of the market make a quick entry important, 2. when the firm needs or is offered opportunity to acquire competent management, 3. when the firm will have to

TABLE 9.4 *Internal Development versus Acquisition*

Synergy		Preferred method	Applicable diversification growth vectors	Exceptions
Start-up	Operating			
Strong	Strong	Internal development	Market development, product development; technologically related horizontal and vertical diversification	1. Timing is of essence 2. Acquisition of good management 3. Acquisition of needed capacity 4. Low-cost product acquisition 5. Stable market shares; no room for new entry
Strong	Weak	Internal development	Unrelated horizontal, and vertical, diversification	
Weak	Strong	Combination of acquisition and internal development		
Weak	Weak	Acquisition	Concentric diversification	1. Timing of no importance 2. Incipient demand 3. No competent firms available 4. High price/earnings
None	None	Acquisition	Conglomerate diversification	

enlarge some of its capacities anyway, 4. when a product developed outside the firm costs less than it would to develop internally,* and 5. as mentioned above, when the market shares in the new industry are stabilized, making it very difficult for a newcomer to take away business from established competitors (as would be the case, for example, in mature industries such as automotive, meat packing, and electrical machinery).

Weak start-up synergy generally makes acquisition preferable. However, if opening synergy is strong – indicating applicable unused, although not critical, capacities – a combination of acquisition and internal development is indicated.

Absence of synergy points to acquisition in most cases. An exception is a situation when the premium on timing is low. This may occur, for example, when the move is being made in support of a very long-term objective and when the competitive advantage is focused on incipient demand.

The middle column in the table relates the method of expansion to the growth vector. The high synergy strategies will usually be pursued through internal development. Synergy can vary in horizontal and vertical diversification and so will the appropriate growth methods. Conglomerate diversification usually calls for acquisition.

SUMMARY

The make or buy decision completes the chain of steps which we have followed in developing a theory and a methodology for strategic decision making. In Chapter 2† the method was described as a 'cascade' of decisions, starting with highly aggregated ones and proceeding toward the more specific. This is demonstrated in Figure 9.2, which presents the overall decision flow in product-market strategy formulation by bringing to-

---

* It is not uncommon to find instances where a large and fully competent organization is better off to buy a development from a smaller firm which can develop it cheaper by virtue of greater flexibility and lower overhead. On the other hand introduction of an externally developed product always raises the danger of N.I.H. (not invented here) reaction and a tendency to reinvent the product internally.

† The reader may wish to review pp. 32–5.

gether and inter-connecting the partial decision flow stages of earlier chapters. As in previous diagrams, the points of management decision are shown by double-lined boxes. The decision flow proceeds from the first preliminary diversification decisions [Stop 1] through three successive preliminary stages based on successively greater information [Stop 2], [Stop 3], and [Stop 4] to the final diversification decision [Stop 5]. Following this, a major decision is made on the firm's organizational strategy (synergy-structure decision) followed by successive decisions on four components of strategy (product-market scope, growth vector, synergy, competitive advantage) and culminated in the make or buy decision.

Another characteristic of the adaptive search method was described as the 'open-ended constraint' property. This is graphically demonstrated in Figure 9.2 through the interplay between the objectives and continuously increasing information about the firm's capabilities and opportunities. Objectives are tentatively selected at the outset and then revised twice during the internal appraisal (see 'revised objectives' box after [Stop 1] and [Stop 3]). They are further reviewed at the point of final diversification decision [Stop 5].

The gap-reduction property is exhibited through repeated comparison of potential and desirable objectives [Stop 1], [Stop 2], 'expansion gap', 'diversification decision', and 'scope and growth vector'.

After analysing the shortcomings of the capital investment theory, we had listed in Chapter 2 some imperatives which must be met by a practical theory of strategic decisions. This list is reproduced below.

1. Include all four, rather than the last two steps of the generalized problem-solving sequence. Emphasis should be on the first two steps, monitoring the environment for changes and searching for attractive product opportunities.

2. Handle allocation of the firm's resources between opportunities in hand and probable future opportunities under conditions of partial ignorance.

3. Evaluate joint effects (synergy) resulting from addition of new product-markets to the firm.

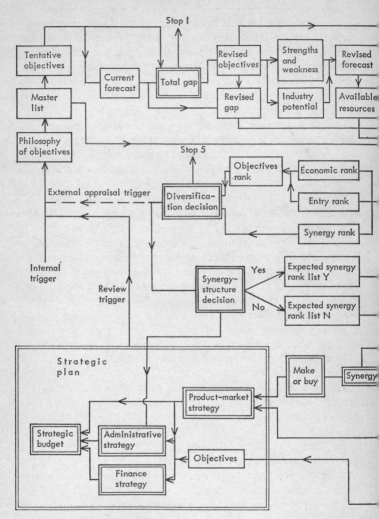

Figure 9.2 Decision flow in product-market strategy formulation.

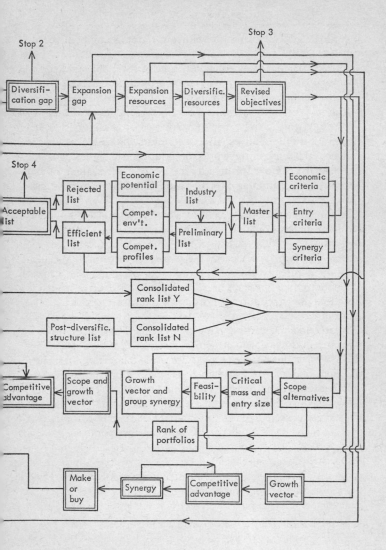

4. Single out opportunities with outstanding competitive advantages.

5. Handle a vector of potentially antagonistic objectives.

6. Evaluate long-term potential of projects even though cash flow projections are unreliable.

The provision for requirement 1. is also demonstrated by Figure 9.2, which can be seen to be focused on a search for and a generation of alternatives. Evaluation and choice stages, in the conventional sense of the words, do not occur until the last stage of the analysis. However, in a more liberal sense, evaluation and choice are a continuing process throughout the respective cascades of the framework.

Although requirement 2., provision for partial ignorance, is not immediately apparent from the diagram, it has conditioned both the theoretical structure and the methodology of the entire approach. Specifically, the two-level method in problem solution (strategy formulation followed by individual project evaluation), the presence of the flexibility objective, and the threshold-goal method of measurement are all due to partial ignorance.

Requirement 3., provision for joint effects, is also a determining influence in the problem structure. Figure 9.2 reflects it through the synergy criteria in external appraisal, the synergy-structure decision, rank of portfolios, and the make or buy decision.

The last two requirements, accommodation to a vector of objectives and provision for measuring the 'unmeasurable' long-term effects, have been handled through the hierarchy of objectives and through the final alternative selection method presented in this chapter.

Our final result is what may be called 'a theory of strategic decisions'. It is built on a series of concepts: objectives (attributes, priorities, and goals), strategy (product-market scope, growth vector, synergy, competitive advantage), present position (measured by forecasts), capabilities (measured by the competence profile), potential (measured by economic potential, cost of entry, and competitive profiles), and synergy (measured by superposition of profiles). Strategy is viewed as an 'operator' which is designed to transform the firm from the present position to the position described by the objectives, subject to the constraints of the capabilities and the potential.

In one sense our formulation falls short of normal requirements of a theory: we do not at this point have unambiguous decision rules at each decision point, which, for example, would make it possible to programme the strategy selection process on a computer. From the point of view of a theoretician this is a defect to be remedied through further research. From the viewpoint of a practical decision maker this may be an advantage, since it permits him to inject into the decisions those intangible situational factors and preferences which are not included in our framework.

If our strategic decision theory were to be compared with others, we suggest that it is a *behavioral theory*, since it deals with decisions by individuals within an organization. It also has strong *economic* overtones, since we assert that the firm's behaviour is profit-oriented, and that institutional characteristics of the firm are dominant in this behaviour, though perturbed and affected by the individual participants.

CHAPTER 10

Uses of Strategy

The fat is in the fire, the die is cast, the jig is up, the goose is cooked, and the cat is out of the bag.

JAMES THURBER

THE PROBLEM

THE strategy formulation framework is completed. Starting with the philosophical issues which underlie objectives, we have traced the process to the point at which the firm commits itself to a specific product-market strategy.

Two tasks remain. The first is to develop a procedure for individual project evaluation and selection. The second is to show how strategy can be used within the overall periodic planning process of the business firm. Before embarking on these, we shall briefly recapitulate and focus the entire process of strategy formulation.

AN OVERVIEW

Figure 9.2 is detailed to a point where we cannot see the 'woods for the trees'. In order to recapitulate and summarize the mainstream of the analysis, we have reduced Figure 9.2 to a schematic in Figure 10.1, which shows only the main building blocks. Using this schematic we shall now briefly retrace the development.

The trigger signal which starts strategic analysis may come about in one of several ways depending on the circumstances of the firm and the far-sightedness of its management. Generally speaking, firms can be divided into three categories: 1. 'reactors' which wait for problems to occur before attempting to solve them, 2. 'planners' which anticipate problems, and 3. 'entrepreneurs' which anticipate both problems and opportunities. Firms in class 3. do not wait for a specific trigger but conduct continual search for strategic opportunities. The post-World

War II business trends have accentuated the need for, and advantages of, anticipation of strategic change.

The immediate reaction to a trigger is to make explicit and/or to review the objectives (1) of the firm. At the present time there is no general agreement on a proper philosophical basis for business objectives. Therefore, our framework for formulating objectives was made adaptable to a variety of different management attitudes, so long as the underlying concept of the firm is

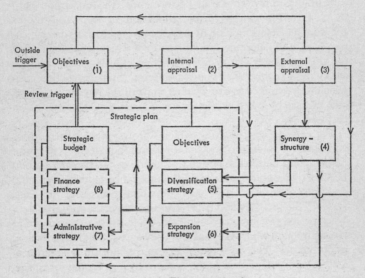

Figure 10.1. The strategic plan.

that of an efficiency-seeking organization which meets the objectives through the mechanism of making and selling goods and/or services.

Real-world business objectives have two characteristics which exert a major influence on the entire process of strategy formulation. The first is that there is not a single objective but rather a vector of objectives, each of which makes competing claims on the resources of the firm. The second is that the threshold-goal values and priorities cannot be set arbitrarily, but must be adjusted in the light of the capabilities and the opportunities of the firm. Figure 10.2 shows this through feedbacks to the objectives box.

Following the initial formulation of objectives, *internal appraisal* (2) is initiated. It is concerned with determining the firm's growth and expansion opportunities within its present product-market posture. It involves a comparison of the potential which exists within the industry with the strengths and weaknesses of the firm. The outcome of internal appraisal is a specification of the improvement in performance (the expansion gap) which the firm will strive for, allocation of resources to this programme, determination of need for diversification (diversification gap), and determination of resources which will be available for this purpose. The decision whether the firm will continue the analysis beyond this point is a milestone management decision which is determined in part by the results of the internal appraisal and in part by whether the firm is a reactor, a planner, or an entrepreneur.

The *external appraisal* (3), which follows, seeks to determine and analyse the field of outside opportunities open to the firm. At this point another major characteristic of the present method becomes evident. Because of partial ignorance, external appraisal does not attempt to deal with individual firms and products. Instead, the analysis is on the level of industries and groups of industries as a preliminary to a later specification of decision and rules (strategy) which the firm will use in its search for individual opportunities. The outcome of external appraisal is a series of lists of industries ranked in the order of their potential for closing the diversification gap and a definitive management decision on whether the firm will diversify.

Before a specific diversification strategy can be selected, another major management decision is made. This is whether and to what extent the firm will vary its organizational *structure* and other administrative arrangements in order to take advantage of the joint-effects (*synergy*) potential (4) available in various industries. The decision taken one way or another affects the final ranking of industries on their potential for the objectives of the firm.

Up to this point the analysis consists of ranking opportunities and screening out undesirable or inefficient ones. The result is a number of lists ranked on the respective objectives of the firm. A major and difficult step is now taken of constructing several alternative product-market scopes (portfolios) into which the firm can afford to diversify and ranking these in the order of *overall preference*. Although extensive literature exists on decision theory, it is of only limited assistance here. The final choice is somewhat cumbersome, because it must attempt to provide for a variety of uncertainties and risks which underlie the evaluation of industries. Analysis tells the responsible manager the consequences of different principles of choice; it is not an automatic decision tool for selection of the best opportunity.

Following the choice of product-market scope, additional components of strategy are selected: the growth vector, the competitive advantage, and the synergy component. Each is designed to sharpen the firm's focus on opportunities which hold the best promise for fulfilling the objectives. This component selection process proceeds in parallel for the *diversification* (5) and the *expansion* (6) substrategy. At the termination the two are added up to produce the total product-market strategy of the firm. Before this can be implemented several important steps and decisions must be taken.

The first is a make or buy decision on the preferred method of growth and expansion. The alternatives of acquisition and expansion are weighed in the light of the objectives, the strategy, and the resources of the firm. The result is a choice of the modes of growth and a resource allocation to each. This decision has profound influence on the internal activities of the firm and the administrative arrangements.

Secondly, an *administrative strategy* (7) must be formulated to establish rules for the organizational evolution of the firm. It is partly predetermined by the synergy-structure decision and the make or buy decision; it needs to be elaborated further into specific organizational relationships and provisions for growth of organizational resources. For example, a major part of the latter is a strategy for expansion and training of management cadres.

Thirdly, a *financial strategy* (8) is needed which will specify the rules and means by which the firm will seek to finance growth and expansion. A decision of major importance is the division of the firm's cash inflow between payment of dividends and reinvestment into the firm. This decision is clearly influenced by the other strategies and, in turn, has a major impact on product-market strategy. Thus, both the finance and the administrative strategy are influenced by, and in turn influence, the product-market strategy. In the preceding analysis we have used this interdependence several times. Thus, the resource projections and limitations (which are determined in major part by the finance strategy) were used in both external and internal appraisal to set overall limitations on strategic activity. Later, the same constraint was used in determining the feasibility of product-market scopes. The synergy-structure decision which has a major effect on product-market strategy is a key part of the administrative strategy.

There is much more to the formulation of these two strategies. Each deserves an analysis comparable in length to the analysis of the product-market strategy presented in this book.

As Figure 10.1 shows, the respective strategies, combined with the objectives, are used to produce a strategic budget and a strategic plan. We defer a discussion of this to a later section and next concern ourselves with the use of strategy and objectives in evaluation of individual projects.

PROJECT EVALUATION

It was seen in Chapter 2 that evaluation of product-market opportunities differs from evaluation of capital investment projects. There are two major points of difference.

1. Because of conditions of partial ignorance, product-market projects cannot all be examined at the same time, but have to be evaluated in a continual stream. This evaluation has to take account of:

a. The present product-market position.

b. The projects currently under way.

c. Other projects which are being held in reserve against availability of resources.

d. Potential future projects which may develop within the budgeting period.

2. Because of the multi-dimensional character of objectives and because of shortcomings of measurement and forecasting, evaluation of a project cannot be based solely on a net cash-flow measurement. Other measurements must be added in order to make sure that the opportunity:

a. Meets the objectives.

b. Fits in with the firm's strategy.

c. Is assessed accurately enough to provide for effects not measured by cash flows.

Using the concepts and results of the preceding chapters, we can now construct a method for project evaluation which satisfies all of these requirements. An outline of the method is shown on Figure 10.2. The decision flow in project evaluation is divided into three main parts: 1. screening, 2. preliminary evaluation, and 3. final evaluation.

The first step in screening is to subject the opportunities to the *threshold-goals* (1) test (see Chapter 4). An opportunity which is below the threshold on all of the major dimensions of the objectives is rejected. If it exceeds one of the major goals, it is retained for future study, regardless of whether it passes the subsequent strategy screening. This provision enables the firm to recognize outstanding opportunities which do not fit the current strategy and thus to remain alert to desirable changes in strategy. If the opportunity lies within threshold-goals range, it is subjected to three successive screenings to determine its fit within the *growth vector* (2), its compliance with the *competitive advantage* (3), and the *synergy* (4) strategy components.

Two screening steps follow – one against the *finance strategy* (5), and the other against the *administrative strategy* (6). In each case a determination is made of whether the opportunity is consistent with the overall guidelines for the firm's growth and change.

Preliminary evaluation, similarly to the external appraisal (see Chapter 7), measures the opportunity against *economic* (7), *cost of entry* (8), and *synergy potential* (9) criteria. It was shown earlier (Chapter 8) that full realization of the synergy potential depends on the administrative strategy of the firm. Therefore, the synergy potential is next adjusted by applying the constraints of that

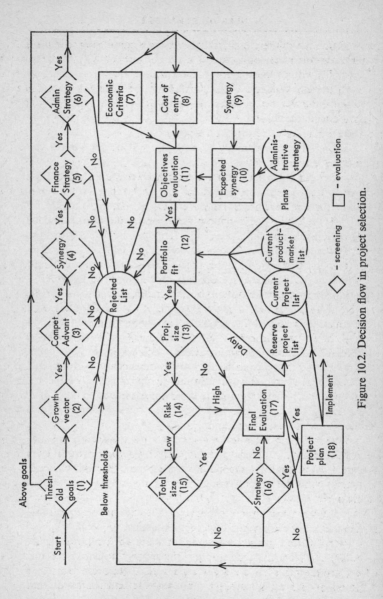

Figure 10.2. Decision flow in project selection.

strategy to produce a measure of *expected synergy* (10). The three criteria ratings are now combined into an *overall project evaluation* (11) with respect to the objectives.

It will be recalled that, because of the manner in which threshold-goals are established (Chapter 4), this is a twofold combined evaluation:

1. Of the merits of the opportunity.
2. Of its relative scarcity.

However, it does not include a comparison with the other projects of the firm. Such comparison is now made in a *portfolio fit* (12). This stacks the new project against the following:

1. The present product-market posture of the firm.
2. The list of currently active product-market acquisitions and development projects.
3. The list of projects not currently active, but which had previously been evaluated, found acceptable, and put 'on the shelf' to await availability of manpower, and other resources.
4. The product-market plan of the firm in the area of the present project.

This comparison leads to one of the following conclusions:

1. Reject the project, because it overlaps with and is not superior to another project already on the books.
2. Provisionally accept the project for implementation.
3. Add it to the reserve list of approved projects.
4. Remove a project on the reserve list and replace it with the same project.
5. Remove an active project – discontinue it and provisionally accept the present project.

If a project is provisionally accepted, it is next screened to determine whether further evaluation is necessary before proceeding with a project plan and with implementation. The screening is on four variables:

1. *Project Size* (13). If the estimated cost of the project exceeds an established minimum, it is assigned to a final evaluation.
2. *Risk* (14). A judgement is made on the basis of combined risk and size as to whether a further evaluation is needed.
3. *Total Size* (15). A small project may generate very large follow-on costs for tooling, facilities, manufacturing start-up,

marketing start-up, working capital needs. A total project investment from start to commercialization is estimated, and if it
exceeds the minimum of 1. above, further evaluation is required.

4. *Strategy Fit* (16). The final screening is only for those outstanding projects which were allowed to by-pass strategy screening in box (1) in Figure 10.2. They are screened now. If there is no
strategy fit, a full final evaluation is needed. Also, depending on
the ramifications of the project, a *strategy review* may be initiated
starting with step (1) on Figure 9.1, or such review may be delayed
pending the outcome of the project.

If no final evaluation is needed, a *project plan* (18) is prepared
and implemented.

Final evaluation consists of determining future cash flows,
investment patterns, and profitability characteristics of the product-market position implied by the project. At this point the
general concepts, techniques, and yardsticks of capital investment
analysis become applicable. If the project involves acquisition
of another firm, a number of specialized techniques of acquisition
evaluation will be applied in addition to profitability evaluation.[110]

In the preceding pages we have been concerned with application
of strategy to evaluation of projects one at a time, as they are
searched out and discovered by the firm. Another and equally
important role of strategy is in the overall periodic planning process of the firm. This, too, involves evaluation of projects – in this
case of the ongoing projects and projects foreseeable at budgeting
times. Going beyond this, strategy is a key to the overall behaviour of the firm in its resource acquisition, allocation, and
conversion processes. The next section discusses this role of
strategy.

A TOTAL PLANNING FRAMEWORK

Business planning has been defined in many ways. Perhaps the
most comprehensive and descriptive definition was given by
Peter Drucker. He defines business planning as

a continuous process of making present entrepreneurial decisions
systematically and with best possible knowledge of their futurity,
organizing systematically the effort needed to carry out these decisions,

and measuring the results of these decisions against expectations through organized systematic feedback.[111]

The definition is in three parts:
1. Making decisions systematically.
2. Preparing programmes for their implementation.
3. Measuring actual performance against the programmes. The relation of Drucker's definition to the content of this book is easy to see, since our entire concern has been with 'making present entrepreneurial decisions' or, to be more precise, with developing rules for making such decisions. To extend our results to Drucker's definition of a *plan* we need to construct a document which will 'organize systematically the effort' for carrying out the decision. We shall call such document a *strategic budget*. We further define a budget as a time-phased schedule for implementation of decisions. It consists of a *performance budget*, which is a schedule of actions to be taken and milestones to be attained, and of a *resource budget*, which is a time schedule of resource commitments (in terms of money, people, facilities, and equity) in support of the performance. A third important part of the budget is a forecast of the results which will be achieved, expressed preferably in terms of a profit and loss forecast and a *pro forma* balance sheet. This might be called a *profit budget*.*

In Figure 10.3 a *strategic plan* is shown to consist of 1. the objectives, 2. the product-market, finance, and administrative strategies, and 3. the strategic budget.

If Drucker's definition of planning and our corresponding definition of the strategic plan are compared with common business practice, a substantial difference would be observed. A majority of business plans consists of what we have defined as

---

* Just as there is no general agreement on what constitutes a plan, there is no agreement on the term budget. Some writers call this part of the plan a *programme* (see, for example, D. Norvick, Ref. 112). More frequently the programme is used synonymously with what we have called a performance budget. This author's preference is close to Norvick's. We suggest that the programme is a tentative unapproved document which becomes a budget when it has been approved and assigned to a particular manager for implementation. This terminology offers management a flexibility for distinguishing between tentative and approved plans.

budgets, without any evidence of the decision analysis required in the first part of Drucker's definition. A small number of plans will contain *assumptions* about factors beyond the firm's control, such as the assumed trends in the economy, industry, political climate, prices. A still smaller number of business plans will add a statement of the decisions which have been made, but again without any description of the analysis which was used to arrive at them. In this respect business planning differs from military

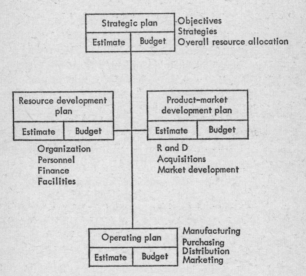

Figure 10.3. Generic structure of plans.

planning, which prescribes that a document titled 'Estimate of the Situation' be prepared in support of all plans.[113] It contains an analysis of alternative strategies and policies which leads to the preferred decisions.

An estimate is useful beyond just being a historical record. As Drucker suggests, the third element of planning is a comparison of the actual results with the forecasts. Such comparisons are often made in firms to take corrective *control* actions when discrepancies occur. However, Drucker's concern appears to be not only with control, but also with use of the comparisons for improvement of *future planning*: improvement in the assumptions, techniques, logic of analysis, search for alternatives, and decision rules. For the purpose of such analysis a budget which is a record of the consequences of decisions is not sufficient. The process of arriving at the decision, such as described in this book, must be recorded.

The difference between common business practice and our definition is further found in the fact that most firms do not prepare a strategic plan which analyses and programmes what we have called strategic decisions. The system of plans is usually confined to operating and administrative budgets. In Chapter 1 we have commented at length on the reasons for omission of strategic decisions from management concern. Lack of interest in the decisions leads to a failure to plan for them.

The preceding comments suggest that most firms need to broaden their planning frameworks in two ways:

1. Through addition of a strategic plan to their system of plans.

2. Through appending a decision analysis to the budgets in each of the plans.

The general framework of a business plan would then look as shown in Figure 10.3. The strategic plan is the key document which gives guidance and allocates resources among the major activities of the firm. This is elaborated in three subordinate plans: a detailed plan for product-market change (product-market development plan), a plan for structure and acquisition of resources (resource-development plan), and a plan for day-to-day running of the firm (operating plan).

Under the plans in Figure 10.3 are shown the principal functional areas included in each. In practice the generic planning structure of Figure 10.3 will have to be adapted to the structure of responsibility and authority. This follows from the fact that, in order to make planning an effective tool of management, the responsibility and the authority for respective budgets should be unambiguously assigned to specific managers.

Three typical planning outlines are shown in Figures 10.4, 10.5, and 10.6 for firms which are organized functionally, firms using the product manager concept, and divisionalized firms. As in all

187

organizational arrangements, none of the three fully meets the criterion presented above. Under the functional organization shown in Figure 10.4, the responsibility for product-market plans is vested in the vice-president for development (in small firms the chairman will double in brass here) while the execution of the plans is assigned to the executive vice-chairman. Thus, responsibility and authority are split down the middle. Under the product line concept of Figure 10.5, product line manager depends on the

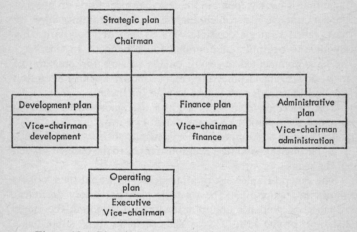

Figure 10.4. Planning system under functional organization.

vice-chairman of operations for manufacturing (and often for distribution). Furthermore, he shares product-market development responsibility with vice-chairman for corporate development. A logical division of this responsibility, as shown in Figure 10.4, is to assign product-market *expansion* to product managers and *diversification* to the vice-chairman for development.

As shown in Figure 10.6, under divisionalized structure a potential conflict exists between the vice-chairman for corporate development and the divisional development managers.*

* This potential conflict has on a number of instances known to the author inhibited the establishment of a corporate development function at a time when it was badly needed.

In order to operate harmoniously, the product-market scope responsibility of each has to be defined clearly. A simple division between expansion and diversification, as in product manager structure, may not be the optimum. Instead the respective areas of responsibility may assign different diversification responsibilities to both. Thus in Figure 10.6 the vice-chairman for corporate

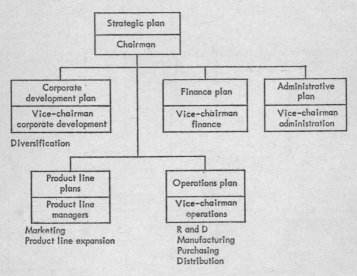

Figure 10.5. Planning system under product line manager organization.

development is made responsible for concentric and conglomerate diversification, and divisional product-market development managers are responsible for expansion, vertical diversification, and horizontal diversification. A further potential problem arises from the fact that the respective division managers are responsible to two corporate officers: to the president for strategic planning and to the executive vice-chairman for operating plans. The dotted lines on Figure 10.5 testify to the very complicated relationships planning for coordinating which arise under divisional organization.

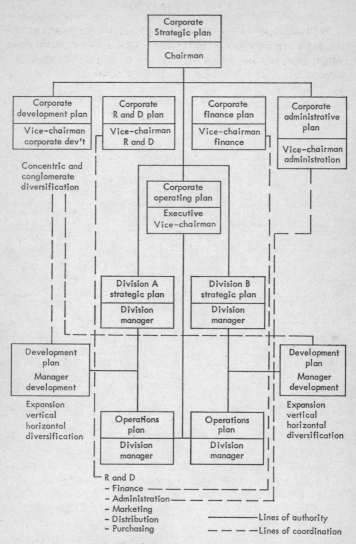

Figure 10.6. Planning under divisional organization.

We have described total business planning only to the extent needed to relate strategy formulation to the larger framework. Much more can and should be said about business planning. An interested reader will find a voluminous literature on the subject.[114]

References

1. R. M. Cyert and J. G. March, *A Behavioral Theory of the Firm*, Prentice-Hall, Inc., Englewood Cliffs, N.J., 1963, chap. III; M. Shubik, 'Information, Risk, Ignorance and Indeterminacy', *The Quarterly Journal of Economics*, vol. 68, pp. 629–40, 1954.

2. Cyert and March, op. cit. (Ref. 1).

3. A. D. Chandler, Jr, *Strategy and Structure*, The M.I.T. Press, Cambridge, Mass., 1962.

4. A. P. Sloan, Jr, *My Years with General Motors*, Doubleday & Company, Inc., Garden City, N.Y., 1964.

5. See, for example, W. Beranek, *Analysis of Financial Decisions*, Richard D. Irwin, Inc., Homewood, Ill., 1963.

6. Beranek, op. cit. (Ref. 5); E. Solomon, *The Theory of Financial Management*, Columbia University Press, New York, 1963.

7. H. A. Simon, *The New Science of Management Decision*, Harper & Row, Publishers Incorporated, New York, 1960.

8. Beranek, op. cit. (Ref. 5), p. 27.

9. *a*. Series of *Fortune* articles on American companies (1960–1963).

b. G. A. Steiner, *Managerial Long-range Planning*, McGraw-Hill Book Company, New York, 1963.

c. M. E. Mengel, 'Integrated Product Planning: From Idea to National Distribution', American Management Association, Marketing Series, no. 101, pp. 3–20, 1957.

d. 'Developing Profitable Product Lines: A Case Study', American Management Association, Research and Development Series, no. 1, pp. 27–50, 1956.

e. 'Meeting the Problems of Rapid Expansion: A Presentation by Texas Instruments, Incorporated', American Management Association, General Management Series, no. 185, pp. 14–52, 1957.

f. R. A. Rich, 'Product Planning: The Benefits of an Integrated Approach', American Management Association, Marketing Series, no. 98, pp. 3–14, 1956.

g. A.M.A. Conference Handbook, *Mergers and Acquisitions: For Growth and Expansion*, published for distribution at the A.M.A. Special Finance Conference, 31 October–2 November 1956, New York.

h. 'A Case Study in Corporate Acquisition', American Management Association, Financial Management Series, no. 115, 1957.

i. W. A. Songer, 'Organizing for Growth and Change', American Management Association, General Management Series, no. 171, 1954.

j. H. R. Lange, 'Expansion through Acquisition, Implementing Long-range Company Planning', Stanford Research Institute, Menlo Park, Calif. (Speech given before Industrial Economics Conference, San Francisco, 21–22 January 1957.)

k. F. E. Larkin, 'Long-range Planning at W. R. Grace and Company', American Management Association, Management Report 3, pp. 54–60, 1958.

l. H. E. Chiles, Jr, 'Tying Sales Planning to Over-all Company Objectives', American Management Association, Marketing Series, no. 94, pp. 8–14, 1955.

m. W. B. Harrison, 'Long-range Planning in a Dynamic Industry', American Management Association, Management Report 3, pp. 47–53, 1958.

n. W. E. Hill and C. H. Granger, 'Long-range Planning for Company Growth', *The Management Review*, vol. 45, pp. 1081–92, December 1956.

o. B. Payne and J. H. Kennedy, 'Making Long-range Planning Work', *The Management Review*, vol. 47, no. 2, pp. 4–8, 73–9, February 1958.

p. P. V. Manning, 'Long-range Planning of Product Research', American Management Association, Research and Development Series, no. 4, pp. 54–67, 1957.

q. E. W. Reilley, 'Planning the Strategy of the Business', *Advanced Management*, vol. 20, no. 12, pp. 8–12, December 1955.

r. W. E. Hill, *Planned Product Diversification*, William E. Hill Company, New York.

s. W. F. Rockwell, Jr, 'Planned Diversification of Industrial Concerns', *Advanced Management*, May 1956.

t. M. Smith, 'How to Initiate Effective Long-range Planning', American Management Association, *Management Report* 14, pp. 69–78, 1958.

u. S. Thompson, 'How Companies Plan', American Management Association, *Research Study* 54, 1962.

10. T. A. Andersen, H. I. Ansoff, F. E. Norton, and J. F. Weston, 'Planning for Diversification through Merger', *California Management Review*, vol. 1, no. 4, pp. 24–35, Summer, 1959.

11. *a.* H. I. Ansoff and J. F. Weston, 'Merger Objectives and Organization Structure', *Review of Economics and Business*, August 1962, pp. 49–58.

b. H. I. Ansoff, 'A Model for Diversification', *Management Science*, vol. 4, no. 4, pp. 392–414, July 1958, reprinted in Thomas L. Berg and Abe Shuschman (eds.), *Product Strategy and Management*, Holt, Rinehart and Winston, Inc., New York, 1963, pp. 288–309.

12. *a*. P. F. Drucker, 'Business Objectives and Survival Needs: Notes on a Discipline of Business Enterprise', *The Journal of Business*, vol. 31, no. 2, pp. 81–90, April 1958.

b. P. F. Drucker, 'Long-range Planning: Challenge to Management Science', *Management Science*, vol. 5, no. 3, pp. 238–49, April 1959.

13. F. F. Gilmore and R. G. Brandenburg, 'Anatomy of Corporate Planning', *Harvard Business Review*, vol. 40, no. 6, November–December 1962.

14. C. H. Kline, 'The Strategy of Product Policy', *Harvard Business Review*, vol. 33, no. 4, July–August 1955.

15. T. Levitt, 'Marketing Myopia', *Harvard Business Review*, vol. 38, no. 4, pp. 45–56, July–August 1960.

16. D. Novick, 'Planning Ahead in the Department of Defense', *California Management Review*, vol. 5, no. 1, pp. 35–42, Summer, 1963.

17. T. A. Staudt, 'Program for Product Diversification', *Harvard Business Review*, vol. 32, no. 6, pp. 121–31, November–December 1954.

18. *a*. G. A. Steiner, 'Making Long-range Company Planning Pay Off', *California Management Review*, vol. 4, no. 2, Winter, 1962.

b. G. A. Steiner, *Managerial Long-range Planning*, McGraw-Hill Book Company, New York, 1963.

19. S. Tilles, 'How to Evaluate Corporate Strategy', *Harvard Business Review*, vol. 41, no. 4, pp. 111–21, July–August 1963.

20. J. F. Weston, 'A Framework for Product Market Planning', presented at the 8th Annual International Meeting of The Institute of Management Sciences, Brussels, Belgium, 26 August 1961.

21. H. Fayol, *General and Industrial Management*, Sir Isaac Pitman & Sons, Ltd, London, 1959.

22. Chandler, op. cit. (Ref. 3).

23. Sloan, op. cit. (Ref. 4).

24. Cyert and March, op. cit. (Ref. 1), chap. 2.

25. FM 101–5, Department of the Army Field Manual, Staff Officers Field Manual, Staff Organization and Procedure, Government Printing Office, Washington, D.C., 1954.

26. H. I. Ansoff, 'A Quasi-analytic Method for Long Range Planning', presented at the First Symposium on Corporate Long Range Planning, The Institute of Management Science, College on Planning, 6 June 1959, and 6th Annual International Meeting, The Institute of Management Sciences, Paris, France, 9 September 1959.

27. G. A. Busch, 'Prudent-manager Forecasting', *Harvard Business Review*, vol. 39, no. 3, pp. 57–69, May–June 1961.

28. H. A. Simon and A. Newell, 'Heuristic Problem Solving', *Operations Research*, vol. 6, no. 1, pp. 1–10, January 1958.

29. Simon, op. cit. (Ref. 7) p. 2.

30. W. Reitman, 'Heuristic Decision Procedures, Open Constraints and Structure of Ill Defined Problems', in M. Shelly and G. Bryan, *Human Judgment and Optimality*, John Wiley & Sons, Inc., New York, 1964, chap. 15.

31. H. Markowitz, *Portfolio Selection: Efficient Diversification of Investments*, John Wiley & Sons, Inc., New York, 1959.

32. An excellent summary of Clarkson's approach can be found in E. Feigenbaum and J. Feldman (eds.), *Computers and Thought*, McGraw-Hill Book Company, New York, 1963. A full treatment is in G. P. E. Clarkson, *Portfolio Selection: A Simulation of Trust Investment*, Prentice-Hall, Inc., Englewood Cliffs, N.J., 1962. The Ford Foundation Doctoral Dissertation Series 1961 Award Winner.

33. Simon, op. cit. (Ref. 7), p. 5.

34. Levitt, op. cit. (Ref. 15).

35. W. Reitman, in Feigenbaum and Feldman, op. cit. (Ref. 32), chap. 2.

36. Ansoff, op. cit. (Ref. 26).

37. H. I. Ansoff, 'A Quasi-analytic Approach to the Business Policy Problem', presented at the 11th Annual International Meeting, The Institute of Management Sciences, Pittsburgh, Pa, 13 March 1964; to be reprinted in *Management Technology*.

38. Simon and Newell, op. cit. (Ref. 28).

39. Simon, op. cit. (Ref. 29).

40. W. R. Reitman, *Cognition and Thought: An Information Processing Approach*, to be published by John Wiley & Sons, Inc., New York, 1965.

41. A. King McCord, 'Management by Objectives', presented at the 14th Annual Award Dinner, Duquesne University Chapter, Society for Advancement of Management, 10 May 1962.

42. H. Granger, 'The Hierarchy of Objectives', *Harvard Business Review*, vol. 42, no. 3, pp. 63–74, May–June 1964.

43. See, for example, Thompson, op. cit. (Ref. 9u).

44. R. N. Anthony, 'The Trouble with Profit Maximization' *Harvard Business Review*, vol. 38, no. 6, pp. 126–34, November–December 1960.

45. M. Kestenbaum, 'The Essential Components of Business Planning', *Planning the Future Strategy of Your Business*, American Management Association, New York, 1956, p. 54.

46. For a critique of micro-economic theory see Cyert and March, op. cit. (Ref. 1), chap. 3; M. Shubik, 'Approaches to the Study of Decision-making Relevant to the Firm', *Journal of Business*, vol. 34, no. 2, April 1961; Anthony, op. cit. (Ref. 44).

47. Solomon, op. cit. (Ref. 6), chap. 2.

48. Beranek, op. cit. (Ref. 5).

49. W. J. Baumol, *Business Behaviour, Value and Growth*, The Macmillan Company, New York, 1959.

50. Drucker, op. cit. (Ref. 12*a*).

51. F. Abrams, 'Management Responsibilities in a Complex World', in T. H. Carroll, *Business Education for Competence and Responsibility*, University of North Carolina Press, Chapel Hill, N.C., 1954.

52. F. Abrams, op. cit. (Ref. 51); R. F. Stewart, *The Strategic Plan*, Long Range Planning Service, Stanford Research Institute, Menlo Park, Calif.

53. D. Cater and M. W. Childs, *Ethics in a Business Society*, Harper & Row, Publishers, Incorporated, New York, 1954.

54. Sloan, op. cit. (Ref. 4); Chandler, op. cit. (Ref. 3).

55. E. S. Mason, 'The Apologetics of Managerialism', *Journal of Business*, January 1958, pp. 1–11.

56. Cyert and March, op. cit. (Ref. 1).

57. Drucker, op. cit. (Ref. 12*a*).

58. H. A. Simon, 'On the Concept of Organizational Goals', *Administrative Science Quarterly*, vol. 9, no. 1, June 1964.

59. Solomon, op. cit. (Ref. 6), chap. 2.

60. A theoretical expression for the procedure is easy enough to write. See, for example, Ansoff, op. cit. (Ref. 11*b*).

61. P. F. Drucker, *The Future of Industrial Man*, The John Day Company, Inc., New York, 1942.

62. G. M. Kaufman, *Statistical Decision and Related Techniques in Oil and Gas Exploration*, Prentice-Hall, Inc., Englewood Cliffs, N.J., 1963.

63. J. F. Weston, *Managerial Finance*, Holt, Rinehart and Winston, Inc., New York, 1962, chap. 5, pp. 82–98.

64. Cyert and March, op. cit. (Ref. 1), p. 26.

65. J. M. Keynes, 'The End of Laissez-faire' (1926), republished in *Essays in Persuasion*, London, 1931, pp. 314–15.

66. Cyert and March, op. cit. (Ref. 1), chap. 3, particularly p. 40.

67. Beranek, op. cit. (Ref. 5), chap. 2, p. 12.

68. H. D. Koontz and C. J. O'Donnell, *Principles of Management*, 2nd ed., McGraw-Hill Book Company, New York, 1959, p. 45.

69. Sloan, op. cit. (Ref. 4), pp. 42–3 and 58–9.

70. Cyert and March, op. cit. (Ref. 1), p. 35.

71. Combined action or operation, as of muscles, nerves, etc. Webster's New Collegiate Dictionary, G. & C. Merriam Company, Springfield, Mass., 1961.

72. Andersen et al., op. cit. (Ref. 10).

73. Staudt, op. cit. (Ref. 17).

74. Kline, op. cit. (Ref. 14); H. I. Ansoff, 'Strategies for Diversification', *Harvard Business Review*, vol. 35, no. 5, pp. 113–24, September–October 1957; 'Strategies for Diversification', *Harvard Business Review*, vol. 35, no. 5, September–October 1957; reprinted in David W. Ewing (ed.), *Long-range Planning for Management*, Harper & Row, Publishers, Incorporated, New York, 1958, pp. 459–86; reprinted in Edward C. Bursk and John F. Chapman (eds.), *New Making Tools for Managers*, Harvard University Press, Cambridge, Mass., 1963, pp. 309–33; Tilles, op. cit. (Ref. 19); Gilmore and Brandenburg, op. cit. (Ref. 13).

75. Levitt, op. cit. (Ref. 15); Chandler, op. cit. (Ref. 3); Tilles, op. cit. (Ref. 19); Brandenburg, op. cit. (Ref. 13); and Ansoff, op. cit. (Ref. 26).

76. Levitt, op. cit. (Ref. 15).

77. L. C. Sorrell, in W. H. Newman, *Administrative Action*, Prentice-Hall, Inc., Englewood Cliffs, N.J., 1951.

78. S. G. Walters, vice-president of Socony-Mobil's Center Division, in *Time*, vol. 82, no. 5, 2 August 1963.

79. Clarkson, op. cit. (Ref. 32).

80. J. von Neumann and O. Morgenstern, *Theory of Games and Economic Behavior*, Princeton University Press, Princeton, N.J., 1953.

81. Ansoff, op. cit. (Ref. 74); Gilmore and Brandenburg, op. cit. (Ref. 13).

82. Chandler, op. cit. (Ref. 3); Tilles, op. cit. (Ref. 19).

83. Kline, op. cit. (Ref. 14).

84. Chandler, op. cit. (Ref. 3), chaps. 6–8.

85. Sloan, op. cit. (Ref. 4), chaps. 1 and 2.

86. *Ibid.*, chap. 4.

87. Chandler, op. cit. (Ref. 3), chap. 8.

88. The five years with the greatest number of mergers (1946, 1947, 1955, 1956, and 1957) had 2,068 mergers. The first wave (1898–1902) had 2,454 mergers; and the second wave (1926–1930) had 4,838 mergers. Source: R. L. Nelson, *Merger Movement in American Industry, 1895–1956*, Princeton University Press, Princeton, N.J., 1959, p. 29. Recent activity as reported by the *Statistical Abstract of the United States*, 1964, p. 101, shows 635 mergers in 1960, 671 in 1961, 672 in 1963.

89. Staudt, op. cit. (Ref. 89).

90. L. Silberman, 'Corporate Treasurers Get More Venturesome in Investing Spare Cash', *The Wall Street Journal*, 5 November 1963.

91. Ansoff, op. cit. (Ref. 74); Staudt, op. cit. (Ref. 17).

92. *The New York Herald Tribune*, 21 August 1963.

93. Ansoff and Weston, op. cit. (Ref. 11*a*).

94. *a*. 'The Unfinished Job at W. R. Grace', *Fortune*, vol. 63, no. 2, p. 108, August 1963.

b. 'It's No Longer Just Grind, Grind at Norton', *Fortune*, vol. 63, no. 2, p. 118, August 1963.

c. 'When the Crowd Goes One Way, Litton Goes the Other', *Fortune*, vol. 62, no. 2, p. 115, May 1963.

95. Clarkson, op. cit. (Ref. 32).

96. *a*. Andersen et al., op. cit. (Ref. 10).

b. Weston, op. cit. (Ref. 20).

c. National Industrial Conference Board, *Growth Patterns in Industry*, Studies in Business Economics, no. 2, 1952.

97. 'Sonnabend's Sackful', *Fortune*, vol. 58, no. 3, p. 133, September 1958.

98. *Statistical Abstracts of the United States*, 1964, U.S. Department of Commerce, which classifies industries by type.

99. *a*. B. Bock, *Mergers and Markets*, National Industrial Conference Board, Inc., New York, 1964.

b. J. F. Weston, *The Role of Mergers in the Growth of Large Firms*, University of California Press, Berkeley, Calif., 1953.

c. D. D. Martin, *Mergers and the Clayton Act*, University of California Press, Berkeley, Calif., 1959.

100. Ansoff and Weston, op. cit. (Ref. 11*a*).

101. H. I. Ansoff, 'Management Participation in Diversification', Stanford Research Institute Client Conference Report, 25–27 September 1963; Chandler, op. cit. (Ref. 3).

102. Cyert and March, op. cit. (Ref. 1), chap. 5.

103. C. W. Churchman, R. L. Ackoff, and E. L. Arnoff, *Introduction to Operations Research*, John Wiley & Sons, Inc., New York, 1957, chap. 6, pp. 136–53.

104. J. D. Williams, *The Compleat Strategyst*, McGraw-Hill Book Company, New York, 1954.

105. Shubik, op. cit. (Ref. 46).

106. W. T. Morris, *Management Science in Action*, Richard D. Irwin, Inc. Homewood, Ill., 1963.

107. Churchman et al., op. cit. (Ref. 103); R. D. Luce and H. Raiffa,

Games and Decisions, John Wiley & Sons, Inc., New York, 1957; W. T. Morris, *Engineering Economy*, Richard D. Irwin, Inc., Homewood, Ill., 1960.

108. D. B. Hertz, 'Risk Analysis in Capital Investment', *Harvard Business Review*, vol. 42, no. 1, pp. 95–106, January–February 1964.

109. Chandler, op. cit. (Ref. 3), chap. 5; Sloan, op. cit. (Ref. 4), chap. 9.

110. M. F. Gordon, 'The Payoff Period and the Rate of Profit', *The Journal of Business*, vol. 28, no. 4, pp. 11253–11260, October 1955; J. Dean, 'Measuring the Productivity of Capital', *Harvard Business Review*, vol. 32, no. 1, pp. 120–30, January–February 1954; D. F. Folz and J. F. Weston, 'Looking Ahead in Evaluations Proposed Mergers', *N.A.A. Bulletin*, April 1962; M. L. Mace and G. G. Montgomery, Jr., *Management Problems of Corporate Acquisitions*, Division of Research, Harvard Business School, Boston, Mass., 1962; American Management Association Conference Handbook, *Mergers and Acquisitions: For Growth Expansion*, 1956; H. I. Ansoff, 'Evaluation of Applied Research in a Business Firm', in J. R. Bright, *Research Development and Technological Innovation*, Richard D. Irwin, Inc., Homewood, Ill., 1964.

111. Drucker, op. cit. (Ref. 12b).

112. Novick, op. cit. (Ref. 16).

113. FM 101–5, Department of the Army Manual, Staff Officers Field Manual, Staff Organization and Procedure, Government Printing Office, Washington, D.C., 1954.

114. a. Beranek, op. cit. (Ref. 5).

b. Steiner, op. cit. (Ref. 18).

c. Stanford Research Institute. Reports on the Long Range Planning Service, Menlo Park, Calif.

d. Novick, op. cit. (Ref. 112).

e. Drucker, op. cit. (Ref. 111).

f. H. I. Ansoff, 'Planning as a Practical Management Tool', *Financial Executive*, June 1964.

Name Index

Abrams, F., 39
Ackoff, R. L., 154
Andersen, T. A., 29, 83, 127
Ansoff, H. I., 29, 35, 46, 83, 94,
  105, 115, 120, 127, 144, 185, 191
Anthony, R. N., 38
Arnoff, E. L., 154

Baumol, W. J., 38
Beranek, W., 24, 25, 38, 62, 191
Bock, B., 138
Brandenburg, R. G., 29, 94, 105
Busch, G. A., 29

Cater, D., 40
Chandler, A. D., Jr., 19, 22, 29, 40,
  94, 105, 109, 112, 162
Childs, M. W., 40
Chiles, H. E., Jr., 28
Churchman, C. W., 154, 157
Clarkson, G. P. E., 30, 104, 124
Cyert, R. M., 16, 22, 29, 38, 40, 41,
  43, 60, 61, 68, 153, 175

Dean, J., 184
Drucker, P. F., 29, 39, 42, 49, 184,
  185, 186, 191

Fayol, H., 29
Feigenbaum, E. A., 30, 35
Feldman, J., 30, 35
Folz, D. F., 184

Gilmore, F. F., 29, 94, 105
Gordon, M. F., 184
Granger, C. H., 28, 36

Harrison, W. B., 28
Hertz, D. B., 159
Hill, C. H., 28

Kaufman, M., 51
Kennedy, J. H., 28
Kestenbaum, M., 36, 196
Keynes, J. M., 61
Kline, C. H., 29, 94, 105
Koontz, H., 64

Lange, H. R., 28
Larkin, F. E., 28
Levitt, T., 29, 31, 94, 95
Luce, R. D., 157

McCord, A. K., 36
Mace, M. L., 185
Manning, P. V., 28
March, J. G., 16, 22, 29, 38, 40, 41,
  60, 61, 68, 153, 175
Markowitz, H. M., 30
Martin, D. D., 138
Mason, E. S., 40
Mengel, M. E., 28
Mitchell, D. G., 161
Montgomery, G. G., Jr., 184
Morgenstern, O., 105
Morris, W. T., 51, 156

Nelson, R. L., 110
Newell, A., 30, 35
Norton, F. E., 83, 127
Novick, D., 29, 185, 191

O'Donnell, C., 64

Payne, B., 28

Raiffa, H., 157
Reilley, E. W., 28
Reitman, W. R., 30, 35
Rich, R. A., 28
Rockwell, W. F., Jr., 28

201

Subject Index

MORE ABOUT PENGUINS
AND PELICANS

Penguinews, which appears every month, contains details of all the new books issued by Penguins as they are published. From time to time it is supplemented by *Penguins in Print*, which is a complete list of all books published by Penguins which are in print. (There are well over three thousand of these.)

A specimen copy of *Penguinews* will be sent to you free on request, and you can become a subscriber at 4s. for a year's issues (with the complete lists) if you live in the United Kingdom, or 8s. if you live elsewhere. Just write to Dept. EP, Penguin Books Ltd, Harmondsworth, Middlesex, enclosing a cheque or postal order, and your name will be added to the mailing list.

Note: *Penguinews* and *Penguins in Print* are not available in the U.S.A. or Canada